DATE DUE

Mary Wollstonecraft

Twayne's English Authors Series

Sarah Smith, Editor

Tufts University

TEAS 381

MARY WOLLSTONECRAFT
(1759–1797)
Courtesy of National Portrait Gallery, London

Mary Wollstonecraft

By Moira Ferguson
University of Nebraska-Lincoln

and Janet Todd
Rutgers University

Twayne Publishers • *Boston*

Mary Wollstonecraft

Moira Ferguson
Janet Todd

Copyright © 1984 by G. K. Hall & Company
All Rights Reserved
Published by Twayne Publishers
A Division of G. K. Hall & Company
70 Lincoln Street
Boston, Massachusetts 02111

Book Production by John Amburg

Book Design by Barbara Anderson

Printed on permanent/durable acid-free
paper and bound in the United States of
America.

Library of Congress Cataloging in Publication Data

Ferguson, Moira.
     Mary Wollstonecraft.

     (Twayne's English authors series; TEAS 381)
     Bibliography: p. 147
     Includes index.
     1. Wollstonecraft, Mary, 1759–1797—Criticism
and interpretation.   I. Todd, Janet M., 1942–
II. Title.   III. Series.
PR5841.W8Z67   1984   828'.609   83-18342
ISBN 0-8057-6867-X

For
Marc Emil Krasnowsky
and
James Lynn

Contents

About the Authors

Moira Ferguson was born in Glasgow, Scotland, and took a B.A. at the University of London and a Ph.D. at the University of Washington. She is an associate professor of English at the University of Nebraska-Lincoln and former chairwoman of women's studies. She has been a fellow of the Henry E. Huntington Library and has received an American Council of Learned Societies Award and an American Association of University Women Founders Fellowship.

Her scholarly articles and reviews have appeared in such journals as *Philological Quarterly, Minnesota Review, Signs, English Language Notes, Romantic Movement, Wordsworth Circle, Victorian Studies*, and *Women's Studies International Forum*. She is the compiler and editor of *First Feminists: British Women Writers 1578–1799* (1983). She is currently preparing a study of women's protest writings in the seventeenth and eighteenth centuries.

Janet Todd, fellow of Sidney Sussex College, Cambridge, was born in Llandrindod-Wells, Wales. She took a B.A. at the University of Cambridge and a Ph.D. at the University of Florida. From 1964 to 1967 she taught in Ghana, mainly at the University of Cape Coast, and from 1972 to 1974 at the University of Puerto Rico. Since then, until 1983, she was professor of English at Rutgers University. She has been the recipient of NEH and ACLS awards and of a Guggenheim Fellowship.

Her books include *In Adam's Garden: A Study of John Clare's Pre-Asylum Poetry* (1973), *A Wollstonecraft Anthology* (1977), *Women's Friendship in Literature* (1980), and, with M. Marshall, *English Congregational Hymns in the Eighteenth Century* (1982). Her scholarly articles and reviews have appeared in journals such as *Signs, Yale Review*, and the *Times Higher Education Supplement*. She is the editor of the *Women & Literature* series, the latest volume of which is *Jane Austen: New Perspectives* (1983). She is completing an encyclopedia of British and American women writers of the eighteenth century.

x i

Preface

The Mary Wollstonecraft revival began slowly. The first good modern biography by Ralph Wardle caused little stir when it appeared in the early 1950s. Before 1960 Wollstonecraft would have been remembered (if at all) as vaguely connected with the poet Shelley, to whom her daughter Mary Wollstonecraft Godwin was married; even today she is so often identified with her daughter that many people think the mother wrote *Frankenstein*. But in the 1960s, a decade in which the women's liberation movement developed national prominence, contemporary scholars recuperated women writers as well as pioneer theorists of feminism, and so rediscovered Wollstonecraft and her momentous document, *A Vindication of the Rights of Woman* (1792). A new edition of this work was issued in the late 1960s. Four major Wollstonecraft biographies by Margaret George, Eleanor Flexner, Claire Tomalin, and Emily Sunstein followed. Good, reasonably priced editions of her individual writings, a bibliography of her works, as well as an anthology and a collected edition of her letters have already appeared.

In this introduction to Wollstonecraft we consider her works. We concentrate on the bulk of her early, middle, and late writings, which disclose not merely her range, intellectual force, and personal appeal, but her political vision and philosophical eclecticism. In addition, we relate her works to her life and note the stages of her struggle to think and act as an independent woman in an age that discouraged such efforts.

The two authors collaborated throughout this book and discussed and formulated each of its sections. Chapters 1, 2, 3, 7, 8, and 9 are, however, primarily the work of Moira Ferguson, and Chapters 4, 5, and 6 primarily the work of Janet Todd. We received a combination of helpful advice, information, and valuable criticism from the following people whom we gratefully thank: Professors Kathleen Blake and Malcolm Brown of the University of Washington-Seattle; Leila Charbonneau of Seattle; Ann Gerike and Willis Regier of Lincoln, Nebraska; Professor Gary Kelly of the University of Alberta, Edmonton; and two biographers of Wollstonecraft, Emily Sunstein of Philadelphia and Professor Ralph Wardle of Creighton University, Omaha, Nebraska. There are also a number of individuals who generously contributed at various stages, especially Catherine Yamamoto of the University of Nebraska-Lincoln who worked on the final preparation. We would also like to acknowledge the courtesy and assistance of the officers and staffs of the Carl H. Pforzheimer Library, Vassar College Special Collections, especially Frances Goudy, the British Library, the Bodleian Library, the University Library of Cambridge, the Firestone Library Rare Books Room of Princeton University, the Douglass College Library of Rutgers University, and the University of Nebraska-Lincoln Love Library. For typing we are especially grateful to Gloria Cohn of the Douglass College English Department, and LeAnn Messing and Cid Donnelly-Nixon of the University of Nebraska-Lincoln English Department.

Moira Ferguson

University of Nebraska-Lincoln

Janet Todd

Rutgers University

Chronology

1759 Mary Wollstonecraft born April 27 in London. Her father, Edward John Wollstonecraft (born 1736), and mother, Elizabeth Dickson (c. 1740), were married in 1756. Their oldest child, Edward (Ned), was born in 1757. Other children: Henry Woodstock (1761); Elizabeth (Eliza) (1763); Everina (Averina) (1765); James (1768); and Charles (1770).

1775 Meets Fanny Blood.

1778 Leaves home to become a paid companion to Mrs. Dawson in Bath.

1781 Returns home to nurse her mother.

1782 Mother dies (April 19). Goes to live with Fanny Blood and family. Eliza marries Meredith Bishop (probably October 20).

1783 Eliza's daughter born (probably August 10).

1784 Asked to tend her sister Eliza during postpartum breakdown (January); removes Eliza from Bishop's house. With Fanny Blood and Eliza, establishes school at Islington, moving soon to Newington Green; Everina joins them. Meets Dr. Richard Price and Dissenters (first exposure to antiestablishment ideas).

1785 Consumptive Fanny Blood marries Hugh Skeys in Lisbon in February. Wollstonecraft goes to Lisbon for birth of Fanny's child in November. Fanny dies in childbirth.

1786 Returns to London. The school fails and the sisters disperse. Writes *Thoughts on the Education of Daughters.* Hired as governess to Kingsborough children in Ireland. Stays briefly at Eton College.

1787 Completes *Mary, A Fiction* in Ireland; dismissed by Kingsboroughs when they go to Bristol. Returns to London and her sympathetic publisher, Joseph Johnson. Hired as translator and reader (and later as reviewer and editorial assistant) for Johnson's forthcoming *An-*

alytical Review; thus becomes one of the few women involved in radical publications. Writes *The Cave of Fancy, or Sagesta* and *Original Stories from Real Life* in second half of year, and completes *The Female Reader*, all published by Johnson.

1788–1790 From self-taught French, German, Dutch, and Italian, translates works that include Necker's *Of the Importance of Religious Opinions*, Salzmann's *Elements of Morality for the Use of Children*, and Madame de Cambon's *Young Grandison*.

1790 In answer to Edmund Burke, writes *A Vindication of the Rights of Men*, published under her own name in the second edition. Takes in seven-year-old Ann (relative of Hugh Skeys) as foster daughter, who stays until second half of 1792. Begins writing *A Vindication of the Rights of Woman* in September. Briefly meets William Godwin in November.

1792 *A Vindication of the Rights of Woman* is published. Sets off for Paris with Johnson and Henry and Sophia Fuseli, all of whom turn back; emotional crisis with Henry Fuseli. Leaves for Paris alone in December.

1793 Meets Gilbert Imlay. Conceives her first child in August. Imlay registers her at U.S. embassy as his wife for protection during the French Revolution. *The Emigrants* is published (probably written by Imlay, although Robert Hare makes a case for Wollstonecraft's authorship).

1794 Daughter Fanny is born (May 14) in Le Havre. Finishes *An Historical and Moral View of the Origin and Progress of the French Revolution, and the Effect it Has Produced in Europe*, which Johnson publishes in London.

1795 Returns to London with Fanny in April. Imlay indifferent. First suicide attempt in May. Travels with Fanny to Scandinavia in June. Returns in September. Second suicide attempt in October.

1796 *Letters Written During a Short Residence in Sweden, Norway, and Denmark* published by Johnson.

1797 Marries Godwin (March 29). Continues work on *The Wrongs of Woman, or Maria.* Plans a book called *Letters on the Management of Children.* Second daughter, Mary, is born (August 30). Dies following childbirth (September 10).

Chapter One

The Background and the Life

Early Life

Mary Wollstonecraft inherited enterprise and independence from her paternal grandfather, Edward Wollstonecraft. He was a self-made man with a shrewd business sense, who forged a career as a master weaver, leased property from the Worshipful Company of Goldsmiths in Spitalfields, London, built thirty blocks of houses, rented out the property, and amassed a fortune. His youngest son, also named Edward, began working life as an apprentice silk weaver to the elder Wollstonecraft and continued as a master weaver until 1765, when his father died.[1] By this time, the son was married to Elizabeth Dickson, formerly from "a good family" in Ballyshannon, Ireland, who bore seven children. Mary Wollstonecraft, the second child and eldest daughter, was born April 27, 1759.

After receiving his moderate inheritance, her father abandoned his craft for the more socially prestigious life of a gentleman farmer. This caused the Wollstonecraft family, steadily increasing in size as the fortune dissipated, to move seven times in the next decade, including a long stay from 1768 to 1774 in Beverley, Yorkshire.[2] As the father's economic failure hastened a personal deterioration, his wife and children became victims of his uncontrollable fits of rage, spurred by frustration and drunkenness. By 1768 the young Mary, in her own testimony, stood watch "whole nights at their chamber-door," waiting to defend her mother from Edward Wollstonecraft's brutalities.[3] As a result, her life developed into "one cry for justice,"[4] as Virginia Woolf described it. With the dwindling away of his inheritance, her father began to expropriate the money settled on his daughters, which in turn made Mary feel obliged to surrender her legacy, and along with it, any chance of the early independence she coveted. Her future fretting over money matters and her constant attacks on the practice of primogeniture stemmed from unpleasant memories of these times as much as from her own impoverished existence.[5]

This short recital records the facts of Mary Wollstonecraft's early life. Very little about the female side of either her mother's or her father's family has come to light. Her mother must be credited with giving her daughter the run of the Yorkshire moors and, by her often pathetic situation, with allowing young Mary to watch and analyze, and so learn to distrust marriage and to value independence and pluck.

During the long spell in Yorkshire she attended the county school and shared lessons from the schoolmaster father of her close friend Jane Arden—her only formal education. Wollstonecraft's occasional correspondence with Jane Arden touched on deeply felt concerns about relationships and feelings, about flirtation, petty jealousy, and allied matters. Yet until much later her letters disclosed next to nothing about her frightening home life. As an adult, Mary Wollstonecraft was unable to maintain such an artificial division.[6]

In 1775 the family moved to Hoxton on the outskirts of London. There Wollstonecraft began the battle for the independence that eluded her almost to her death; she demanded from her parents but was refused a room of her own. At the same time, she made friends with their elderly next-door neighbors, Mr. and Mrs. Clare, who allowed her to use their library and read and study in their home. Through them she met their friend, Frances (Fanny) Blood, who powerfully influenced her growth toward independent womanhood. At eighteen and two years Wollstonecraft's elder, the well-versed Fanny Blood had already learned to sew, sketch, paint fine water colors, play the piano, and converse fluently on a variety of subjects, all desired accomplishments for young gentlewomen. These skills also helped her to assume a large part of the responsibility for her own family's welfare. Eager to advance herself intellectually, Wollstonecraft "adopted" Fanny Blood as her mentor. "Before the interview was concluded," William Godwin writes of the first meeting between the women, "[Mary] had taken, in her heart, the vows of an eternal friendship."[7] To Jane Arden, Wollstonecraft wrote that "to live with this friend is the height of my ambition." Since these emotional references to Fanny Blood nowadays raise the question of lesbianism in Wollstonecraft's life, it should be noted that women frequently wrote passionately and erotically to each other.[8] For example, the loverlike stance of Anna Howe toward Clarissa in Richardson's *Clarissa* was both a model for women and a reflection of practice. No exception, Wollstonecraft used the language of tender eighteenth-century "romantic friendship" with Fanny Blood.

Just after her death, Wollstonecraft wrote on May 1, 1786, to Fanny's brother George Blood: "She was indeed George my best earthly comfort—... I am only anxious to improve myself and so run my race that I may met (*sic*) my poor girl where sorrow and sighing shall be no more."[9] Twenty years after Fanny Blood's funeral, Wollstonecraft still eulogized her friend, her feelings undampened by the passage of time: "The grave has closed over a dear friend, the friend of my youth; still she is present with me and I hear her soft voice warbling as I stray over the heath."[10]

In the summer of 1777 the Wollstonecraft family returned to Walworth in South London, possibly living in a house owned by Thomas Taylor, the Platonist.[11] They remained there together until 1778 when the nineteen-year-old Wollstonecraft defied parental directives by accepting employment in the fashionable city of Bath as a live-in companion to a rich, demanding widow, Mrs. Dawson. She at first welcomed the position because it allowed her a measure of autonomy. (To chaperone was one of the few options for paid employment that lower middle-class women could socially afford.) Eight years later, however, in her first publication entitled *Thoughts on the Education of Daughters*, she described this experience as a nightmare of tyranny and humiliation.[12] A request from home to nurse her dying mother interrupted this bold, early bid for an independent career. From the autumn of 1781 until the spring of 1782, the combination of Mrs. Wollstonecraft's protracted illness and persistent favoritism toward Ned, the eldest son and heir, and her father's punishing behavior exhausted Mary Wollstonecraft's energy and patience, and embittered and alienated her.[13]

When her mother died in 1782, Wollstonecraft moved in with the poverty-stricken Blood family, who now lived at Walham Green, South London. There for about two years she cheerfully contributed what she could earn. Undeterred by penury or the example of Mrs. Blood who had become almost blind from years of daily sewing, Wollstonecraft sewed until she became ill from eyestrain, while Fanny Blood painted watercolors for a pittance. Fanny Blood described this desperate situation (depicted fictionally by Wollstonecraft in her only complete novel, *Mary, A Fiction*) when she wrote to Everina about

a plan for gaining independence together: "Half a guinea a week . . .
would just pay for furnished lodgings for three persons to pig together. As for needle-work, it is utterly impossible they would earn
more than half a guinea a week between them, supposing they had
constant employment which is of all things the most uncertain. Mary's
sight and health are so bad that, [sic] I'm sure she never could endure
such drudgery. . . . As for what assistance they could give me at the
paints we might be ruined before they could arrive at any proficiency
in the art."[14]

Because she had for so long suffered a general depression and
nervousness, often mentioned in her correspondence, the friendship
and unaccustomed tranquility of life at the Bloods far outweighed
any physical difficulties, but her treasured peace was soon shattered
by another family catastrophe. Her younger sister Eliza had married
Meredith Bishop fourteen months earlier. In mid-January 1783, when
her daughter was five months old, Eliza suffered a postpartum nervous
collapse. Thereupon Wollstonecraft, with some assistance from her
other sister, Everina, and Fanny Blood, kidnapped Eliza to separate
her from her home, her husband, and her baby. A letter from Mary
to Everina captured the gravity of the situation: "But to make my
trial still more dreadful, I was afraid, in the coach, she was going
to have one of her flights, for she bit her wedding ring to pieces. . . .
I hope B[ishop] will not discover us, for I could sooner face a lion. . . .
Bess [Eliza] is determined not to return."[15]

Aware of the sacrosanct role that marriage played in her society,
Wollstonecraft predicted the probable consequences of her action. "I
knew I should be the . . . shameful incendiary," she confided to Everina, "in this shocking affair of a woman's leaving her bed-fellow."[16]
Her prophecy proved accurate since her reputation never recovered
from this act even long after her death. Questionable as the abduction
of Eliza and the abandonment of the baby (possibly in deference to
the legal situation in which a baby "belonged" to the father)[17] might
have been, the incident also underlines Wollstonecraft's confidence in
her own convictions, her loyalty to loved ones, and her clear-minded
control and strong will, all of which later enabled her to flout convention privately and in her published writings. For the time being,
however, she resigned herself to the notoriety that her refusal to con-
form to eighteenth-century values forced upon her.

The Newington Green Experiment

Propelled by financial need and inspired by the Arden sisters who had opened an Academy of Female Education at Bath in 1781, Wollstonecraft planned a day school for private pupils. The first attempt to open a school at Islington in North London was unsuccessful. Fanny, Eliza, and Mary Wollstonecraft were then joined by Everina at nearby Newington Green; from the start, the second venture fared well enough to support all four women and to qualify them for future careers as governesses. They were aided by Sarah Burgh, a Newington Green resident, who suggested they accommodate lodgers and who used her influence to bring in about twenty pupils during the first few weeks. Shortly afterwards, the consumptive Fanny Blood set out for Lisbon to meet her fiancé Hugh Skeys, married him there in February 1785, and almost immediately became pregnant. In September, at an inopportune time for the school, Wollstonecraft felt compelled to join her friend, and with characteristic impulsiveness, set sail for Lisbon. When she arrived, Fanny Blood was already in labor and subsequently died.

Fanny Blood's death caused Wollstonecraft to reassess her future. She had known that her friend's frail, tubercular constitution could scarcely withstand pregnancy, and that bearing a child in that condition had largely contributed to her death. She told William Godwin that around this time she made a vow against marriage for herself; by this she would preserve her own health and well-being, and help abate the horrible memory of Fanny Blood's death.[18] That vow also preserved the sense of loyalty she felt to their past friendship.

Another example of Wollstonecraft's developing independence and courage occurred on her return trip from Lisbon. When the ship's captain refused to help stranded French soldiers in the Bay of Biscay, an enraged Wollstonecraft threatened to expose his inhumanity as soon as they reached England, at which point the captain capitulated. With the expression of the sailors' gratitude ringing in her ears, she sailed the rest of the way home experiencing a small compensatory triumph amid her personal grief.

Back in England she found their school was disintegrating, for Everina and Eliza lacked Mary's perseverence, tact, and sense of responsibility. She responded to this disastrous loss of their collective livelihood with a mixture of nervous disorders, determination, and patient resignation, lately familiar themes in her letters. She excused her sisters by explaining, "They are not calculated to struggle with the world."

Regardless of the failure, the experience had left her with a new and important group of acquaintances. In founding the school at Newington Green, Wollstonecraft had met the circle of rational Dissenters who had made that part of North London their home. This community included Richard Price, a moral philosopher and minister; his frequently visiting friend Joseph Priestley, the scientist; the Reverend John Hewlett; and Sarah Burgh, all of whom welcomed Wollstonecraft to their intellectual and social bosom. Already firmly unorthodox except in her religious beliefs, she was attracted to these radicals who, like herself, opposed with clearly articulated concern the muddled complacency about the social order. Indeed Sarah Burgh, widow of the philosopher and educator James Burgh who wrote *The Dignity of Human Nature* (1754) and *The Art of Speaking* (1762), became Wollstonecraft's most supportive companion. Mrs. Burgh worked at keeping alive her husband's ideas in *Thoughts on Education* (1747), in which forty years earlier he had probed the question of female education. Through such friends and acquaintances Wollstonecraft encountered fresh ideas about education, pedagogy, and rhetoric. These caused her to reexamine her religious standpoint, at that time in loose conformity with the tenets of broad-church Anglicanism, and to systematize or generalize her sense of injustice. Sarah Burgh, in particular, might have functioned as a sounding board for Wollstonecraft's ideas and may have helped her to realize she could progress beyond teaching to writing.

First Writings: Adventure in Ireland

After the school failed, Hewlett encouraged her to write an educational tract, which he hoped would interest his publisher friend Joseph Johnson. The work's full title was *Thoughts on the Education of Daughters; with Reflections on Female Conduct, in the More Important Duties of Life* (1786), its content a transformation of Wollstonecraft's personal beliefs and experiences into the beginning sketch of a political philosophy. The public took slight notice. Spontaneously generous again where the Bloods were concerned, Wollstonecraft sent the whole family to Ireland with the ten guineas she received for writing the book, since she judged their need to recover from Fanny's death far in excess of her own.

To eke out a living and repay mounting debts, she accepted the position of governess to Lord and Lady Kingsborough's three daughters, a post obtained through Mr. and Mrs. John Prior of Eton, also friends of Price. It would be a disastrous period for the proud, poor Wollstonecraft, and she approached it with no enthusiasm. "I by no means like the proposal of being a governess—I should be shut out from society . . . as I should on every side be surrounded by unequals."[19] After an inconvenient and fruitless delay in Eton awaiting her employers' children—her first taste of their thoughtless behavior—Wollstonecraft left London in late 1786 to take up her position on the two-thousand-acre estate in Mitchelstown, County Cork, Ireland, one hundred and seventy miles from Dublin. Despite the Kingsboroughs' progressive management of the estate, Wollstonecraft found in their personal life only idleness, and it reinforced her earlier unfavorable impressions of the privileged and fashionable at Bath and Eton.[20] The care Lady Kingsborough lavished on lapdogs at the expense of her children shocked and grieved Wollstonecraft. In *A Vindication of the Rights of Woman* she later painted a distinctly unflattering portrait of such a woman; for the time being, she contented herself with a description of Lady Kingsborough's unpleasant traits (and her own personal pride) in a letter to Everina:

> I find her still more haughty and disagreeable. . . . Indeed, she behaved so improperly to me once, or twice, in the Drawing room, I determined never to go into it again. I could not bear to stalk in to be stared at and her *proud* condescension added to my embarrassment, (sic) I begged to be excused in a civil way. . . . I had too, another reason, the expense of hair-dressing, and millinery, and would have exceeded the sum I chose to spend in those things . . . just at this juncture she offered me a present, a poplin gown and petticoat, I refused it . . . she was very angry.[21]

More agreeably, she established soundly based, affectionate relationships with her wards, especially Margaret, the eldest, of whom Wollstonecraft spoke in a letter to Johnson as someone who "may be allowed to cheer my childless age." "At any rate," she went on, "I may hear of the virtues I may not contemplate—and my reason may permit me to love a female."[22] She appears again to have singled out a female friend for special attention, possibly approaching a re-enactment of her love for Fanny Blood, when Lady Kingsborough severed that relationship, in part out of jealous pique over her daughter's attachment to the governess. In future years, when public aspersions were cast upon Wollstonecraft for corruption of these Kingsborough charges, Margaret Kingsborough, then Lady Mount-cashel, staunchly defended her former governess.[23]

When she was not tutoring and worrying about her "nerve disorders," Wollstonecraft tried to further her career as an author by reading contemporary British and European works. "I am now reading for my own private improvement," she informed Everina. Her tastes were increasingly discriminating, including Jean-Jacques Rousseau's *Emile*, Hugh Blair's "Lectures on Rhetoric and Belles Letters," Charlotte Smith's poems, and Stéphanie de Genlis's letters on education. She also wrote her first novel entitled *Mary, A Fiction*, which at first glance would pass as just another slim, sentimental work of fiction. Yet its surface orthodoxy belies a number of provocatively fresh ideas, heralded by a preface of remarkable literary insight. It also reveals in painful detail Wollstonecraft's self-pitying concept of her more melancholy moments and her dissatisfaction with, as well as her love for, the dead Fanny Blood.

Wollstonecraft cherished few illusions about her tenure as governess: "I long since imagined that my departure would be sudden,"[24] she later revealed to Everina. Thus she was at least psychologically prepared when Lady Kingsborough discharged her after ten months' service.

Philosophy in Transition

Having few prospects left as a teacher, Wollstonecraft returned to her publisher Joseph Johnson in London in hopes of launching a literary career for herself. "I am then going to be the first of a new genus," she announced to Everina. She judged well. Johnson, a risk-taker of some vision who had long befriended and published the unorthodox, invited her to live at his home and to work for him as a writer, translator, editorial assistant, and reviewer for his forthcoming journal, the *Analytical Review*.[25] This monthly, founded by Johnson and his colleagues in May 1788, consisted of long reviews of major works, followed by shorter notes on less important writings. Since it was liberal and radical in focus, many reviled it as jacobin. Probably gratified by Johnson's confidence in her, Wollstonecraft kept this job, with some gaps, until the end of her life. She left her reviews unsigned, as the rest of the staff did, presumably because of editorial policy, although Ralph Wardle and others have persuasively speculated about her contributions.[26]

Wardle gives to Mary Wollstonecraft all reviews signed 'M' or 'W' as well as a series of anonymous reviews followed by one with an 'M' or 'W'. On grounds of style and content he also gives her 'T' reviews. He comes up with 412 reviews, some only a sentence long. His views are opposed by Derek Roper who suggests only 204 and Eleanor Flexner who doubts even 212 'M' reviews since *Analytical* signatures were rather random.

Wollstonecraft's reviews covered a wide variety of subjects, including sermons, romances, travelogues, and children's books, but between 1788 and 1792 she concentrated on reviews of fiction and educational works. In the latter, as she discussed principles of education for women particularly, she praised writers who respected women's minds but decried those who labeled women "over-grown children." Her fiction reviews showed the same tendency. She castigated "flimsy" female novels that gave young girls a literary vehicle of escape into a fantasy world, calling instead for more mature literature that would inculcate morality and flex the intellect.[27] These reviews of 1788–1792 link the earlier, more conservative ideas that Wollstonecraft expressed in her educational works and the more radical views of the two *Vindications*. They document her apprenticeship in the reviewing craft, and her early intellectual influences such as that of the feminist historian and theorist Catherine Macaulay, whom she ardently admired.

About this time she worked on a children's book, attempted another fictional tale, compiled an anthology for women, and rather ambitiously began to translate works from French, Dutch, and German.[28] The anthology of prose and verse, entitled *The Female Reader*, offered students as well as teachers and governesses a typically eighteenth-century comprehensive program of intellectual, moral, social, and religious development.[29]

Gradually, during the course of a trial period as an aspiring writer, debater, and thinker, Wollstonecraft came to treat Johnson's home as the hub of her social life. She could challenge and exchange ideas in an absorbing intellectual atmosphere with such company as William

Godwin, the radical philosopher; his friend Thomas Holcroft, political activist, playwright, translator, and novelist; Henry Fuseli, the Swiss painter and writer; William Blake, the visionary painter, printmaker, and poet; Anna Laetitia Barbauld, the educator and author; Thomas Christie, the radical Scot, who cofounded the *Analytical Review*; and Thomas Paine, the celebrated radical activist-philosopher whose works on behalf of revolutionary North America were so influential.

These new socioprofessional activities introduced Wollstonecraft, who had been raised an Anglican, to a more controversial religious outlook, although according to Godwin she subscribed to religious beliefs "little allied to any system of forms . . . [and] almost entirely of her own creation." By her most prolific period as a reviewer in 1791, when Johnson published *A Vindication of the Rights of Men*, she was denouncing religion as a people's soporific, a "fable . . . on which priests have erected tremendous structures of imposition to persuade us that we are naturally inclined to evil."[30] Godwin records in his *Memoirs* that she abandoned regular church attendance in favor of a "less constant" practice about 1787 (21-22).

When she began to write for the *Review*, Wollstonecraft consciously avoided controversial issues because of her indifference to politics. Even after her visit to Portugal, her analysis extended to little more than an attack on the Catholic Church; she scarcely probed the role of the government or the political implications of the backwardness she found there. The next two years, however, brought her to vehement advocacy of the goals of the early French Revolution, so much so that except for her advanced feminist views, her radical analysis of contemporary society became indistinguishable from that of Thomas Paine. (Later in Paris they both cast their lot with the moderate girondists against the more radical jacobins.)

Simultaneously, her educational reviews bore witness to her advancing awareness of women's secondary status. She not only criticized Rousseau's theories of education, which she had formerly praised in personal correspondence, but to Lord Chesterfield's pronouncement in *Letters to His Son* that women "are only children of a larger growth," she retorted that precisely this kind of indoctrination had rendered members of her sex "artificial, useless characters."[31] In a fourteen-page review of Catherine Macaulay's *Letters on Education*, she adopted a staunchly supportive tone, and in *A Vindication of the Rights of*

Woman, published two years later, she repeated almost verbatim the
following quotation from Macaulay's *Letters*: "I know of no learning,
worth having, that does not tend to free the mind from error, and en-
large our stock of useful knowledge."[32]

This reassessed political outlook, in addition to her loyal commitment to friends, was unexpectedly tested in 1790 following the publication of Edmund Burke's *Reflections on the Revolution in France*.
The work was an attack on the view argued by her Dissenting friend
and mentor Richard Price, who supported the French Revolution and
hoped for its extension to Britain. Her almost instant rebuttal of
Burke's rebuttal, which she named *A Vindication of the Rights of Men*,
quickly provoked hostile public reaction.

Some of Wollstonecraft's feminist points soon received a more complete statement in her best-known work, *A Vindication of the Rights
of Woman*, which was published in three volumes between the end
of 1791 and March 1792. Curiously enough, she chose this moment
of publication for what appeared to be a well-meaning act, adoption of
Ann, the orphaned niece of Hugh Skeys's second wife.[33] Certainly
Wollstonecraft felt herself ready for the responsibility at the time,
although she surrendered it in November 1792; perhaps she hoped to
ward off potential criticism of her social and domestic conduct in 1791,
which she might have anticipated would follow the attack on her
ideas.

In enlightened circles the *Rights of Woman* attracted unequivocal
praise and admiration. Despite the early somewhat favorable reception, however, by the time the conservative, postrevolutionary reaction
set in, her book seemed dangerously inflammatory. Wollstonecraft
had proved that she could argue her well-formulated insights about
social inequities with a vigorous self-confidence, and to such opponents
of her ideas as Horace Walpole and Hannah More, she burst forth as
a force to reckon with, one of the "philosophizing serpents we have in
our bosom," they declared, a "hyena in petticoats."[34] Politically, Wollstonecraft had arrived.

First Loves

Members of Johnson's circle, including the Swiss painter Henry
Fuseli to whom she became strongly emotionally attached, afforded
deep friendship to Wollstonecraft. These relationships provided her

with a steady intellectual diet as well as strength against censure. Abandoning the old black dress that had earned her a disparaging comment from Fuseli—a "philosophical sloven," he scoffed—she powdered her hair and cultivated a more stylish appearance. She read widely in music, painting, and aesthetic theory to sharpen her mind and conversation. Moreover, she began to realize how much "catching-up" she needed to hold her own at Johnson's. By the end of 1792 she had freely adapted Christian Gotthilf Salzmann's *Elements of Morality*, published her two *Vindications*, sat for her portrait (evidence of her growing fame), and had proposed to an astonished Henry and Sophia Fuseli a social, but not sexual, ménage à trois. Their unceremonious rejection of that offer led her to consider leaving England. So, with wounded feelings and the public barking at her heels, Wollstonecraft put her political ideas into practice in 1792 by going to Paris at the pitch of revolutionary ferment. At first she had set out with Johnson and the Fuselis but turned back when events in Paris seemed inauspicious; now she went on her own: "As I go alone neck or nothing is the word," she bravely asserted to her friend William Roscoe. ". . . I am still a Spinster on the wing. At Paris, indeed, I might take a husband for the time being."[35]

Another result of Wollstonecraft's growing fame was her occasional success in placing her brothers and sisters in good positions. As a case in point, Roscoe helped Charles in his passage to the United States at this time. The second *Vindication* and her removal to France, however, marked a juncture in her sibling relationships; after these events, she became more detached from her family.

Once in France, Wollstonecraft began one of her most neglected works, *An Historical and Moral View of the Origin and Progress of the French Revolution*, in which she disclosed her increasing sense of the importance of understanding history and historical process. By this time Wollstonecraft's thinking not only recognized the subjugated condition of women as more intractable than it had seemed when she wrote her second *Vindication*, she was alive also to the horrors of slavery. Among her acquaintances, William Roscoe and Helen Maria Williams created strong public sentiment against slavery, which Wollstonecraft herself clearly opposed. (The selections in *The Female Reader* alone testify to this.)

In France Wollstonecraft met a dashing North American adventurer-businessman named Gilbert Imlay, who shared many of her liberal views. Soon after they met in April 1793, *The Emigrants* was published, an extremely sentimental three-volume epistolary novel about North America proving that liberated people are superior to slaves. Set in rural Pennsylvania, it tells of a poor young woman wooed by a devoted lover. After hitches due to Native American Indians and her wicked sister, the couple wed and receive wealth. The ending has them setting off to found a utopian community on the banks of the Ohio River. When the girondists fell in May 1793, British citizens were no longer safe in Paris. For Wollstonecraft's protection Imlay registered her as his wife at the American embassy, and on May 14, 1794, she gave birth to their daughter Fanny, named for Fanny Blood. Six months after the birth, the first volume of her history of the French Revolution was published. Industry yoked to intensity of living had by now established itself as a lifelong pattern.

About the same time, Wollstonecraft sank into seriously low spirits owing to Imlay's marked indifference, but she wrote to him often when his business affairs separated them. These personal letters were later published as *Letters to Imlay* (1798) and *Letters Written During a Short Residence in Sweden, Norway, and Denmark* (1796) (hereafter called *Letters from Sweden*). Written both for Imlay and for publication, they record the relationship while they exhibit Wollstonecraft's need for love and security. Obviously, as a dependable, courageous woman she could capably function in all kinds of critical situations; she could moreover effect change and take responsibility for directing her own life and the lives of others; for emotional sustenance and happiness, however, she counted on secure but passionate relationships. Despite her constant advocacy and praise of self-reliance and independence, she found herself writing to Imlay, "my own happiness wholly depends on you" (*PW*, 1:139) and "it is necessary to be in good-humor with you, to be pleased with the world" (*PW*, 1:136). Thus Wollstonecraft's love letters prove her to be a woman very much swayed by emotions once they absorbed her. Indeed, her letters to Imlay have begun to earn her a reputation as one of the most tender love correspondents in the language, a woman deeply touched by and in touch with her feelings, unafraid to express them extravagantly, unabashed by lavish sentiments.

As Imlay withdrew his affection, she shifted into a different, more frenzied emotional gear. At first when his affections waned she burst with fury and resentment; finally, she despaired to the point of a suicide attempt in May 1795. She exploded when her scheme, "one of the calmest acts of reason" (*PW*, 1:246), was thwarted. To help her convalesce from that abortive attempt, Imlay arranged for her, her maid Marguerite, and Fanny to go on a long trip to Sweden, Norway, and Denmark, where from June to September 1795 she served as his business agent. *Letters from Sweden* sparkle with some of her finest prose in which her political insights affirm a shrewdly discriminating judgment. At times transcending her deep sadness, she rhapsodizes about the resuscitating powers of nature in terms that anticipate William Wordsworth: "In solitude, the imagination bodies forth its conceptions unrestrained. . . . These are moments of bliss. . . . Summer disappears almost before it has ripened the fruit of autumn—even, as it were, slips from your embraces, whilst the satisfied senses seem to rest in enjoyment.[36]

Wollstonecraft could not prolong these intervals of happiness. She returned to London to try for a reconciliation with Imlay only to find him living with a young actress. In October 1795 she attempted suicide again by first soaking her bulky clothing in the torrential rain and then leaping into the River Thames from Putney Bridge. Two fishermen, unexpectedly close by, managed to save her after she had become unconscious. A letter to Imlay expresses her disappointment at the failure of her earlier suicide attempt and succinctly identifies a central truth about her relationship with him and about her life in general: "An accumulation of disappointments and misfortunes seem to suit the habit of my mind" (*PW*, 1:249). Throughout her letters of fifteen years she had intermittently expressed a desire for death as a means of breaking free from personal miseries. That desire reached its climax in her precipitous plunge from Putney Bridge.

William Godwin

After the disastrous mismatch with Imlay, Wollstonecraft reencountered William Godwin, this time with "friendship melting into love." As an isolated radical who defied the mainstream and was subject to scorn and ridicule in the press and in public, Godwin resembled her. His familiarity with public censure helped him understand Wollstonecraft's emotional needs, and with a rock-solid affection he strengthened her in the wake of her traumatizing experiences. Where Imlay had been casual in his feelings, Godwin offered love with commitment. Where Imlay had been inconsiderate and boorish, Godwin offered sense and delicacy. When Wollstonecraft betrayed old fears by testing Godwin's feelings in querulousness born of emotional insecurity, he apprehended the truth that lay beneath the surface. Without naming the problem, he confronted this insecurity and cautioned her not to allow her feelings to "tyrannise" over her: "Estimate every thing at its just value."[37]

The commerce-minded Imlay had no conception of the heights that Wollstonecraft dared to scale; the politically minded Godwin was attracted to such courage and strength. A lone woman, the outstanding feminist in England in an epoch of progressive radicalism, Wollstonecraft had borne a child out of wedlock and had tended and provided for her daughter. All the while she had remained financially independent and emotionally and intellectually intense. Godwin's response so suited Wollstonecraft that with his companionship her emotions finally complemented her intellectual maturity. Self-fulfillment, she had come to realize, demanded a merger of thought with feeling. As she delighted in her second pregnancy, she was also busy drafting her political novel, *The Wrongs of Woman, or Maria*, as well as a sketch of pediatrics entitled *Letters on the Management of Infants*, and a short analytical piece on aesthetics. She was also delighting in a great number of friendships with noted women of the time, including Eliza Fenwick and Mary Hays.

Wollstonecraft became pregnant in December of 1796. On March 29, 1797, probably to ease her life and public position and despite Godwin's publicly stated political principles, the two were married at St. Pancras Church in London. At age thirty-seven she finally rejoiced in the tranquil relationship that had so long eluded her. But Mary Wollstonecraft had mere months left to enjoy such hard-won happiness. Because of inept medical care while she was giving birth to her second daughter on August 30, 1797, the placenta remained in her body for several days, and grew gangrenous. The child survived to become Mary Shelley, future author of *Frankenstein*; but eleven days after the birth, Mary Wollstonecraft Godwin died.

Chapter Two

Early Writings on Education

The State of Female Education

By 1786, when Mary Wollstonecraft wrote her first educational tract, women were viewed as emotionally and financially dependent, expected to trust their domestic and financial security to men.[1] The same status was reaffirmed by the law that subsumed a woman's identity within that of her husband. When a woman married and thus became one with her husband, she lost her legal identity for her own protection and benefit. Neither her property after marriage nor her children belonged to her. On top of that, divorce, even for wealthy women, was exceedingly difficult.[2]

Educational theory and practice reflected that position.[3] In the late seventeenth century Bathsua Makin had run an intellectually oriented academy for girls, and in the late seventeenth and early eighteenth centuries Mary Astell and Daniel Defoe had proposed establishments of rigorous learning for women. By the late eighteenth century, however, most education for girls was carried on in fashionable day and boarding schools, which more resembled the school of feminine accomplishments of Mrs. Salmon's at Hackney, offering no classics, some French and Italian, and much catechism, than they did the intellectual institutions experienced by Makin and imagined by Astell.[4]

As she grew up, Mary Wollstonecraft must have known of these modish schools that catered to daughters of the middle class, some of which went so far as to have young females walk around with boards attached to neck irons as a prescription for good deportment. Affluent families who could afford private tutors generally declined to hire one for a daughter alone; the best educational advantage a girl could possess was a brother whose tutor she might share. A daughter had need only of a good marriage; that was her first responsibility, her primary goal in life. The basic requirements for attaining this goal were a fetching appearance (and the schools laboriously instructed females in the use of dress and cosmetics), social graces, and a very limited yet carefully chosen potpourri of facts. This piecemeal program, in addition to a little history, a little reading, and a hefty dose of scripture, became the standard educational diet of daughters being force-fed for the marriage market.

The female poor had no such educational or social ambitions. They were destined by their class to be largely servants or the wives of laboring men, most of whom wanted a good housekeeper, a moral and submissive wife, a respectable mother, and perhaps a manual wage earner.

A few fortunate middle- and upper-class women, for example, Elizabeth Elstob, Mary Wortley Montagu, Elizabeth Carter, Elizabeth and Sarah Robinson, and Anna Seward, were educated and encouraged by male relatives. Other women were encouraged by women. The Bluestockings were intellectual and refined ladies who conversed and corresponded about intellectual and artistic matters. They were an important influence in metropolitan cultural life and they provided an audience and a support system for suitable and acceptable women writers.[5] Wollstonecraft, unconnected with these elevated circles, was helped along between the ages of nine and fifteen by a competent Yorkshire day school. She took advantage of cultured, educated friends such as the Clare family, Fanny Blood, the intellectual Dissenters of Newington Green, and eventually Joseph Johnson's radical circle, to teach and support herself.[6]

Mary Wollstonecraft's Educational Ideas

Wollstonecraft viewed childhood and education as all-important in creating character; the significance of education, in fact, had consciously become a key part of her deepening understanding of the world. From the Dissenters and her own experience she learned the need to develop mental faculties, and she understood that freedom was needed to cultivate reason and to help people achieve fuller humanity. Perhaps the greatest influence of all on her two earliest educational tracts was John Locke's philosophy of education, which stressed the importance of environment and experience.[7]

In *Thoughts on the Education of Daughters* (1786) Wollstonecraft emphasized (as Locke had done in *Some Thoughts Concerning Education*, 1690) the importance of early environment, and the need to treat children as individuals and not small adults and adapt their education to their evolving capacities. In this scheme, education was seen as a process to be pursued rather than a product to be acquired.

Although Mary Wollstonecraft accepted that most women would end up as wives and mothers, she simultaneously stressed the need for females to think, to be critical and intellectually engaged, to learn from experience, and to be fair-minded, compassionate, and well balanced between work and play. Furthermore, she recognized other options. Some of the *Original Stories*, for example, stress the advantages of the single life and the dangers of married life, and indirectly suggest occupations for women. Both *Original Stones* and *Thoughts* also argued that exercise of reason produces virtuous behavior, that experience is the best teacher, and that the mind must question itself and its worth. Wollstonecraft's rationality did not sap her piety; she consistently subscribed, for instance, to the theory of heavenly rewards for earthly tribulations.

These two works combined rationalist and pious approaches to the world and stressed the acquisition of mental and moral knowledge. By encouraging the values of self-respect, independence, and moral and intellectual inquiry, Wollstonecraft meant to improve the socially, intellectually, and physically underprivileged lives of females. Yet, while in *Thoughts* she emphasized child development, the consideration of one's role in the world, the cultivation of a virtuous life, and thinking for oneself, in *Original Stories* she presented more of a program in moral values for their own sake, by which children could learn their way in a corrupt and unfeeling world. Embittered by her experience as a chaperone, in *Thoughts* she underscored that accomplishments cannot always save impoverished gentlewomen from humiliating careers. In *Original Stories*, on the contrary, she depicted a woman who temporarily had to abandon a career, just as she herself had had to leave her first job as a result of her mother's illness. Nonetheless, Wollstonecraft presented the model of a firm working woman of independent mind, whom parents could respect and from whom children could learn.

In the same period as she wrote *Original Stories*, Wollstonecraft was debating what to include in her anthology, *The Female Reader*. The preface reveals similar intentions: to instruct students in usefulness, cultivate their taste, and sharpen their intellects. In that preface, however, Wollstonecraft revealed more clearly than in *Original Stories* her acceptance of the idea of a private sphere for women. Despite restrictions against women making speeches in public, good conversation like religion, must always be attended to. "Females are not educated to become public speakers or players; . . . But if it be allowed to be a breach of modesty for a woman to obtrude her person or talents on the public when necessity does not justify and spur her on, yet to be able to read with propriety is certainly a very desirable attainment."[8] The ultimate goal and the reward of virtue is to reach true happiness in the kingdom of "a beneficent Father."

To this end Wollstonecraft chose a variety of selections: religious and historical materials; social and moral-based excerpts that decry trivial accomplishments and vanity in females and encourage the virtues, notably modesty; and dialogues to improve speech and intonation. Inclusion of antislavery passages from William Cowper also illuminated Wollstonecraft's own views, common among Dissenters.

In Christian Salzmann's *Elements of Morality*, which she translated in 1790, individuals are cautioned to appreciate good health and the poor are advised that they can have a good life through their own efforts, with charitable help from the rich. The farmer in the narrative, for instance, teaches Mr. Parson to concentrate on honest work, a sound personal economy, and the bare necessities of life. While luxury in its physical manifestations is unaffordable, its concept can nonetheless corrupt. Patience can soften pain, intemperance will disrupt a person's life, suspicion and hatred must be shunned, and people should be satisfied and make the best of their lot—so run the requirements of a good life, according to Salzmann. Shortly after this translation, when she wrote *A Vindication of the Rights of Men*, Wollstonecraft no longer contentedly condoned class divisions within society, but at that time she accepted them, and Salzmann's simple stories closely resemble the message of *Original Stories*. One difference, however, shows Wollstonecraft's increasing political sophistication: her preface enjoins that Native Americans must receive fair treatment.

Throughout these early works Wollstonecraft consistently treated education as the solution to women's mental and physical lack of development and as a sine qua non for independence, equality, and the virtuous life. With Locke and her contemporary Catherine Macaulay, she held that boys and girls possess the same nature and they should

therefore be educated much more soundly and equitably. Both Wollstonecraft and Macaulay abhorred Rousseau's notion that females
were on earth to please males.[10] Educational writers such as John
Fordyce and James Gregory tried to help women along by patroniz-
ing them with friendly, fatherly advice. Gregory even urged a sensible
consideration before embarking on marriage. Fordyce and Gregory
advised and exhorted women to be good helpmates and daughters. Dr.
Fordyce particularly promoted piety and such "retiring graces" as tenderness and timidity, and for variety a light concentration in geography, history, and other branches of polite learning. Dr. Gregory urged
more learning, provided females concealed their knowledge. He raised
connivance to the level of art, his justification being that male
pleasure constituted the main object of female existence.

Wollstonecraft attacked Rousseau, Fordyce, and Gregory in *A Vindication of the Rights of Woman* after she had more fully developed
her ideas on the differences between the sexes. In Chapter 12, "On National Education," Wollstonecraft says boys and girls must be educated together from five to nine. At nine working class boys and girls
"intended for domestic employments or mechanical trades" are separated off, kept together in the morning, and educated for training
(according to gender) in the afternoon. Those "of superior abilities
or fortune," male and female, go on together. The nonconformist
religious views to which she had been exposed when she lived in
Islington further confirmed her belief that sexual differences in education should be eliminated. She came to see that the view of boys as
aggressive and girls as timid (even allowing for differences in physical
strength) fundamentally impeded the female intellectual life. Before
she reached these conclusions, however, well-meant yet pernicious
propaganda about the assigned roles and rights of women filled the
heads of parents and children alike. Wollstonecraft's mild-mannered
early writings on education, while agreeing with some points that she
later castigated, did provide an important contrast at other levels.
They upheld the principle of female education, the female capacity
for reasoning, and the right to a better life, although they tended to
assume—with some indirect exceptions—that a woman would auto-
matically assume the role of wife and mother. The careers that Wollstonecraft wanted opened to women in the second *Vindication* had not
yet been added to her educational agenda.

Thoughts on the Education of Daughters

Thoughts on the Education of Daughters primarily addresses the need for female education; usefulness is the justification. She takes as her material the narrow choices open to herself and other women, in a series of short, loosely connected, essay-like chapters. She then weaves into her experiences the psychological developmental ideas from Locke and David Hartley, ideas about the management of daughters from James Burgh, and spiritual rationalist approaches to the moral intellectual life from Richard Price and orthodox religious writers.

Having recently administered a day school and witnessed parental caprice at first hand, Wollstonecraft had rather keenly begun to understand the importance of rational motherhood and the imitation of mothers by daughters as an indirect, unconscious form of learning. As a consequence, she primarily aims her advice at parents. Her statement on the societal role of women in *The Rights of Woman* could have appeared in *Thoughts*: "Speaking of women at large, their first duty is to themselves as rational creatures, and the next in point of importance, as citizens, is that which includes so many, of a mother."[11] In her own life and writings she never swerved from this reverential view of motherhood, but at the same time she came to respect the right of some women to forego this near-commandment of society.

Thoughts contains Wollstonecraft's advice to parents and daughters about common pitfalls and the need for moral, social, and some intellectual improvement. Since she considers superior motherhood a primary role, much of what she says tends to that end. She insists that cultivation of the mind can offset the humiliating social and domestic situation of females and enable them to trust more to their own judgment. Evidently, she has begun to analyze environment as a principal determinant in the condition of women's lives. Her plea for social and spiritual instruction shows her belief in such familiar eighteenth-century ideas as moderation, obedience, piety, and resignation, control of the passions, benevolence, truth, and love. Above all, her informal program applauds that most admired and encouraged female quality of passivity.

Yet Wollstonecraft's concern to see women educated eventually does challenge Gregory's traditional views. "Reason must ... fill up the vacuums of life; but too many of our sex suffer theirs to lie dormant."[12] Her argument directly relates to her personal experiences at home with her mother, to her job-seeking efforts, and to her exceptional environment at Newington Green, where she noted the respect the Dissenting community accorded women compared to their general treatment in society.

She was well aware of the narrow range of female occupations, since she had tried out most of the popular options for middle-class females. In the chapter headed "Unfortunate Situation of Females, Fashionably Educated, and Left without a Fortune," she shares with the reader perceptions about impoverished women that she had acquired at first hand as companion to Mrs. Dawson. "Few are the modes of earning a subsistance, and those very humiliating. . . . [It] is still worse, to live with strangers, who are so intolerably tyrannical that none of their own relations can bear to live with them" (69-70).

The chapter entitled "Love" unwittingly forecasts her future mésalliance with Gilbert Imlay. "People of sense and reflection," she muses "are most apt to have violent and constant passions, and to be preyed on by them. . . . Perhaps a delicate mind is not susceptible of a greater degree of misery . . . than what must arise from the consciousness of loving a person whom their reason does not approve" (82-83).

Her knowing statement in the chapter on "Matrimony" that "nothing . . . calls forth the faculties so much as the being obliged to struggle with the world" (100), again stems from the school of hard knocks, from what she had observed of married women's lives, and from dissatisfaction with the inequalities with which women contended. Her personal frustration corroborates her empirical data, although by writing this book she makes the point that other women can also write, and thus can engage in similar experiences to their benefit.

Many of Wollstonecraft's early ideas come together in *Thoughts*. Servants are children to be controlled, maternal affection ensues "as much from habit as instinct" (4), environment critically matters, and reason governs the individual. Decrying "external accomplishments which merely render the person attractive" (24), she wants to substitute creative, intellectual activities for social affectations and excesses. She ranks independence of mind paramount. Significantly, in view of her awareness of class distinctions later, she zeroes in on human suffering, demanding that theaters show "the complicated mis-

ery of sickness and poverty, and weep for the beggar instead of the
king. . . . Good will to all the human race should dwell in your
bosoms" (141).

Original Stories

In the two years between *Thoughts* and *Original Stories from Real
Life; with Conversations Calculated to Regulate the Affections and
Form the Mind to Truth and Goodness*, Mary Wollstonecraft's life
diverged uncommonly from the conventional life of an eighteenth-
century unmarried woman. Obliged to abandon the Newington Green
experiment and having set sail across the Irish Sea to work as a governess, she again displayed unusual independence in her decision to
write for a living. As she grappled with her views on society, her
writing enabled her to sort out her ideas and integrate them with her
experiences.

In *Original Stories* she adopts a different pedagogical posture than
she had taken in *Thoughts*, intending the former more as an instruction manual in moral excellence, which offered a working method-
ology and a loose philosophy based on Christian moral values and a
diluted version of lockean rationalist thought. Wollstonecraft's personal experiences in Ireland, where she observed how children needed
to learn and think rather than emulate bad parental models, partly
explains this altered approach. Teaching by questioning, so goes her
method, will lead students to the moral life. Her emphasis on reason,
memory, and the association of ideas, in addition to her developmental
approach, philosophically connects her with Price and Hartley as well
as Locke. The mentor in *Original Stories*, Mrs. Mason, directs students toward finding rational solutions to daily problems, so that her
pupils end up, at least in theory and somewhat superficially, with a
modicum of independence and self-assertiveness. Wollstonecraft has
come to agree with Rousseau (whose *Emile* she read in Ireland)
that the mentor, not just a model, is crucial in fostering the sense of
freedom and independence that encourages learning.

Wollstonecraft outlined to Joseph Johnson her remedial goal and
her audience: "The few judicious [parents] who may peruse my book,
will not feel themselves hurt . . . in a book intended for children. . . .
If parents attended to their children, I would not have written their
stories; for what are books, compared to conversations which affection

inforces."[13] Her approach to this form of corrective training was inspired by the recently conceived genre of children's literature. As early as *Thoughts*, Wollstonecraft had commented on the popularity of moral tales for children: "Little stories about [animals] would not only amuse but instruct at the same time," she said of Sarah Fielding's *Perambulations of a Mouse*.[14]

Using a fictional context, Wollstonecraft employs the same instructional format in *Original Stories*. Mary and Caroline, aged fourteen and twelve, are born to wealthy parents who turn them over as infants to the care of ignorant people. When their mother dies, the father hires Mrs. Mason, "a woman of tenderness and discernment," as tutor. Finding them inadequately educated, Mason rarely leaves their sight and resolves to embed, but in practice dins into them, a sense of the moral life through relentless instruction and example. She outdoes Locke in her insistence on virtue as its own reward. Impressed and intimidated by such an inflexible code and demeanor, the children earnestly, even desperately, seek to please her. They learn the dangers of anger, vanity, lying, and other vices through edifying "original" stories about people who have violated the moral code only to be summarily punished in hideous ways. They learn not only about the sufferings but about the material conditions of the poor. Mrs. Mason demonstrates to them the virtue of an individualist but spirited generosity. Moreover, her humanitarian approach, so fundamental to the book's message, probably means that Wollstonecraft had been influenced by and was promoting the ideas of contemporary philanthropists. Particularly, because of her newly found acquaintances, she may even have been aware of and impressed by the important role women like the Bluestockings were playing in the philanthropic movement.

In her omniscience and ubiquity, Mrs. Mason resembles Emile's tutor, willing to manipulate the children to make her point. Impecunious people function as examples, virtually dehumanized, for example, when Mrs. Mason and her charges go shopping in London. After Caroline has squandered all her money on toys, Mrs. Mason "looked round for an object in distress; a poor woman soon presented herself. . . . Mrs. Mason desired the girls to relieve the family; Caroline hung down her head abashed—wishing the paltry ornaments [toys] which she had thoughtlessly bought in the bottom of the sea. . . . Caroline expected the reproof that soon proceeded from the mouth

of her true friend. I am glad that this *accident* (my italics) has oc-
cured, to prove to you that prodigality and generosity are incompatible.
Oeconomy and self-denial are necessary in every station, to enable us
to be generous, and to act comformably to the rules of justice."[15]
(This rather mechanically administered lesson at the expense of the
humanity of impoverished people became quite a feature of late
eighteenth-century and Victorian Sunday-school literature.) Furthermore, to highlight the dangers of procrastination, Mrs. Mason relates
the agonizing (and preposterous) history of Mr. Charles Townley,
who loses all he has and indirectly causes several deaths because he
carelessly delays. The melodramatic tale also illuminates Wollstonecraft's ideas about traditional morals and raises the issue of women
forced by poverty into unsuitable marriages that affect their mental
health. By extension, marriage itself becomes questionable.

Mrs. Mason hastens to apply the rules of middle-class charity when
she uncovers needy people who know their place. This perhaps reflects a touch of self-pity from Wollstonecraft herself, and possibly
the example of conservative moralists beloved by the Bluestockings,
such as Hannah More and Sarah Trimmer, whom Wollstonecraft had
just met. Mrs. Mason relishes being charitable, provided the recipients
have led lives of impeccable virtue. She instructs Mary and Caroline
that "The poor who are willing to work, have a right to the comforts
of life" (32). William Blake's somewhat severe drawings of Mrs.
Mason for the book may indicate his opposition to these views.[16]

Although Mrs. Mason offends against human sensibility in the
name of enlightenment, in terms of eighteenth-century general practice she remains reasonable, sensitive, and philanthropic. Thus she
seems much like the Mary Wollstonecraft who, in January 1787
wrote of her job in Ireland: "I go to the nursery—*something like*
[her italics] maternal fondness fills my bosom—The children cluster
about me—one catches a kiss, another lisps my long name—while a
sweet little boy, who is conscious that he is a favorite, calls himself
my Son—At the sight of their mother they tremble and run to me for
protection—this renders them dear to me—and I discover the kind of
happiness I was formed to enjoy."[17] This overt affection probably
motivated her later adoption of Ann, who by 1792, however, had been
turned over somewhat unceremoniously to Everina.

Once again Wollstonecraft infuses her writings with personal experiences. Trapped like the trio of Wollstonecraft sisters by marital

or monetary difficulties, unfortunate women provide Mrs. Mason with "examples," and again offer something of a warning against both marriage and the single life of poverty. The indelible, most pitiful autobiographical statement comes from Mrs. Mason herself: "Heavy misfortunes have obscured the sun I gazed at when first I entered life— early attachments have been broken—the death of friends I loved has so clouded my days; that neither the beams of prosperity, nor even those of benevolence can dissipate the gloom; but I am not lost in a thick fog.—My state of mind rather resembles the scene before you, it is quiet—I am weaned from the world, but not disgusted—for I can still do good—and in futurity a sun will rise to cheer my heart— Beyond the night of death, I hail the dawn of an eternal day! I mention my state of mind to you, that I may tell you what supports me" (60-61). These words paraphrase Wollstonecraft's statements in her contemporary correspondence to her sisters.

Additionally, a strong similarity exists between the lives of Wollstonecraft and the character of Anna, an abused schoolmistress: "She had her father's spirit of independence, and determined to shake off the galling yoke which she had long struggled with, and try to earn her own subsistence. Her acquaintance expostulated with her, and represented the miseries of poverty, and the mortifications and difficulties that she would have to encounter. Let it be so, she replied, it is much preferable to swelling the train of the proud or vicious great, and despising myself for bearing their impertinence, for eating their bitter bread;—better, indeed, is a dinner of herbs with contentment. My wants are few. When I am my own mistress, the crust I earn will be sweet, and the water that moistens it will not be mingled with tears of sorrow in indignation" (68). Equally moving is Mrs. Mason's tale of the charge she adopted (as Mary Wollstonecraft was to adopt Ann), who "dispelled the gloom in which I had been almost lost" (73).

Resembling Wollstonecraft again, Mrs. Mason cannot countenance the thought of *not* doing good, since she cherishes her own self-respect; Mrs. Mason might well have written Wollstonecraft's words to Joseph Johnson: "While I live, I am persuaded, I must exert my understanding to procure an independence, and render myself useful. . . . My cares and vexations—I will say what I allow myself to think—do me honour; as they arise from my disinterestedness and unbending principles; nor can that mode of conduct be a reflection of my understanding which enables me to bear misery, rather than self-ishly love for myself alone."[18] Mrs. Mason's continual burrowing into her "own" life for examples repeats Wollstonecraft's practice in *Thoughts*. That experiences build and in turn create knowledge is the message. The sorry situation in which the pupils find themselves reinforces the trusty tenet that environment determines character, but it is reason that reveals this truth.

Wollstonecraft appears to have used Mrs. Mason to correct what she saw as her own failings. "I am a strange compound of weakness and resolution," she informed Johnson at the time. "Till I can form some idea of the whole of my existence, I must be content to weep and dance like a child."[19] Mrs. Mason tries to prevent this kind of immoderate emotion and uncontrolled behavior in her wards. In harmony with the Dissenters' practice of self-examination and criticism, Wollstonecraft consciously or unconsciously instructed herself through her fictional creations. She might also have been appeasing her conscience for her desertion of actual teaching by offering literary instruction through Mrs. Mason to females at large.

Finally, *Original Stories* helped to combat the pernicious influence on children of mothers without morals. Mrs. Mason's farewell comments to Mary and Caroline echo Wollstonecraft's parting words to the Kingsborough children: "I now, as my last present, give you a book, in which I have written the subjects that we have discussed. Recur frequently to it, for the stories illustrating the instruction it contains, you will not feel in such a great degree the want of my personal advice." These words constitute her first act of revenge on Lady Kingsborough for the humiliation and injustice of being dismissed. Wollstonecraft implies that Mrs. Mason's pupils will need their mentor's educational books, since, like the Kingsborough children, they have no parental guidance to speak of.

In these educational works Wollstonecraft proclaims the importance of intellectual and moral growth at the same time as she deplores all forms of vanity that women cultivated; these affectations distorted women's fulfillment as useful social beings, as well as their capacity to be competent, enlightened mothers. Nevertheless, one should not overstress the progressive elements; despite frequent foreshadowings of Wollstonecraft's later analysis, standard eighteenth-century pious morality and ideas do dominate, supported and presented in a clumsy, derivative form.

Her other two educational works of this period are *The Female Reader* (1788), an anthology textbook of prose and verse for young women with an introduction and personal prayers written by Wollstonecraft, and her translation of Christian Salzmann's work in 1788–1790. They reflect the same preoccupations and interests[20] and the same contrast between an intellectual versus a moral program of the other two books. They sketch out a tentative program for moral, spiritual, and intellectual growth; they hint strongly, if only by their existence, that females must be educated; they introduce enlightenment principles in her emphasis on egalitarian treatment for Native American Indians and against slavery in the translation and in the anthology excerpts, respectively.[21] Where Wollstonecraft in *Elements* emphasizes the need to view Native American Indians as our "brothers," in *The Female Reader* she goes further and includes significant passages against slavery.

The importance of all the early educational writings is principally due to the fact that Wollstonecraft's major works developed out of them; they were, in a sense, her intellectual apprenticeship. Moreover, this process of learning to marshall and market her talents, and in so doing building her self-confidence, in turn helped to make the *Vindications* a reality.

Chapter Three

Early Fiction: *Mary, A Fiction* and *The Cave of Fancy*

Although women had earned a living from writing since the Restoration, only drama and the novel attracted professional women writers (as well as readers) in large numbers. The lack of formal requirements and the economic benefits directly contributed to this literary phenomenon.[1]

Back in the 1670s and 1680s Aphra Behn had been the first known woman to earn her living only from writing.[2] Toward the end of her career she wrote prose fiction, including the novel *Oroonoko*. Her contemporaries Hannah Woolley and Bathsua Makin had been paid for their writings without doubt, but they had not had to rely on their literary output as their sole means of subsistence. Later in the seventeenth century, Mary Astell's essays on a variety of intellectual controversies brought her a modest income, while her contemporaries Mary Delarivière Manley, Cathcrine Trotter, and Mary Pix supported themselves for various periods of time (Pix the longest) by writing for the stage. Several other writers such as Jane Barker and Sarah Fyge Field Egerton also received payment for assorted volumes of prose and poetry.

The prohibitively high price of books before 1740 had kept the readership of fiction low and severely curtailed its publication. In the early 1740s, however, with the appearance of the first circulating libraries in London, middle-class women, higher domestic servants, and other assorted groups found reading fiction finally to be within their financial reach.[3] To maintain a good stock and ensure a high turnover, bookseller-publishers encouraged neophyte authors to write. Soon such women as Sarah Fielding and Charlotte Lennox joined the ranks of those who in the 1720s wrote scandal chronicles and sensational romance fictions—Manley and the prolific Eliza Haywood. Manley's extravagant prose enabled her to become the first woman to be decently renumerated for her fiction. Sarah Fielding probably spoke for many in the preface to the first edition of *The Adventures of David Simple* (1744) when she told of the penury that brought her to the novel.

With Fielding in the 1740s and the Bluestockings, whose salons began functioning in the 1760s (and earlier) women were gradually and cautiously entering the literary fray.[4] Sarah Scott, the novelist sister of Elizabeth Montagu, queen of the Bluestockings, maintained a steady income from her novels. In fact, ever since Samuel Richardson wrote *Pamela* in 1740, a novel in the epistolary style that did not demand a rich classical education, women had felt somewhat at ease offering their literary wares to the reading public. Letters had long belonged to the female literary tradition, and epistolary works, by Mary Davys, for example, had preceded *Pamela*. Added to that fact, women themselves now comprised a considerable part of the reading public, so it was not surprising that in 1778 Fanny Burney's *Evelina* could be published to wide critical acclaim.

The knowledge that female readers acquired from the library shelves might well have been the extent of their adult learning, superficial though it was, since the age promoted moral rigor as the goal of female life.[5] Circulating libraries kept expanding, partly in response to this predominantly female readership, often leisured, socially constrained, affluent, and seeking outlets.[6] As large numbers of women became regular customers, they recommended books to one another and compared notes. It was an education in sentiment, escapism, and adventure, and also in female autonomy and the possibilities of earning a living.

As companion to Mrs. Dawson in fashionable Bath from 1784–1786, Wollstonecraft had been well acquainted with the cult of novel reading, so much so that by the time she taught in Ireland she knew that many women like herself had tried to enter fiction's ranks, often by writing their own life experiences. She had employed a similar strategy to break into the educational market—in that case she had transformed her limited experiences into a manual for parents. In both *Mary, A Fiction* and *Thoughts* she wrote what she knew, including personal experiences in both and professional experiences in the latter. The two works were successful in that they brought Wollstonecraft much-needed pounds.

In theme and tone, her first novel resembles earlier schematic and episodic examples of the genre. It also includes her concerns about female education in Mary's search for self-knowledge. At the same time, Wollstonecraft offers a female version of the education in moral sentiment popularized in the previous decade by Henry Brooke and Henry Mackenzie.[7]

Mary, A Fiction combines a tale of spiritual endurance on the domestic scene with a less than conventional love story infused with philanthropic attitudes. A frequently staccato, robotlike dialogue; swiftly changing scenes; and melodramatic, mawkish, and reflective passages are welded to uneven lyrical moments. The whole is partially redeemed by the consistency of the central character who, despite seeming ridiculous at times, often commands both emotional and intellectual sympathy. With hints of epistolary style and even of a travel adventure, *Mary, A Fiction* ends up a helter-skelter mixture of literary possibilities. At the same time, glimpses of female imagination and nature, and of an overly pessimistic sensibility intersect with commentary on every conceivable aspect of the times to provide a window of vision into the complexities of an eighteenth-century girl's adolescence. The disquisition covers humanitarian ideals, questions of moral reformation, primogeniture, filial duty, forced marriage, the influence of nature, the strength of female friendship, insensitive, frivolous motherhood, the right to one's sexuality, the harassment of nervous disorders, sickness, and death, much death. As a complex being, unsubmissive, intelligent, sensitive, and eschewing contemporary ideas about domestic bliss and the happily ever after, the fictional woman clearly reflects her creator. In the end, despite a nod to convention, the subtle force of Mary's will brings the novel to an untempered, incomplete conclusion.

Mary, A Fiction

Turning her back on past literary tradition, Wollstonecraft seeks to be midwife to a "new breed" of thinking heroines. In the preface she says, "In delineating the heroine of this fiction, the author attempts to develop a character from those generally portrayed. This woman is neither a Clarissa, a Lady Gregory, or a Sophie. . . . The author will not copy but will rather show how these chosen few wish to speak for themselves and not to be an echo—even of the sweetest sounds—or the reflection of the most sublime beams. The paradise they ramble in must be of their own creating."[8] Evidently she wanted to endow this heroine with a healthy emotional makeup and an imaginative, well-developed mind.

When Wollstonecraft wrote *Mary, A Fiction* she was an impecunious, nervous, but ambitious young woman. Under the guise of fiction she could write autobiography, a natural preference for a novice writer, while trying to distance herself from her own story. Self-pity frequently breaks through the text, however, forcing the reader to look at the author instead of the character.

The book fictionally records Wollstonecraft's deep but unsatisfying relationship with her first love, Fanny Blood (Ann of the story). Beyond this soars her desire to display a woman who could stand on her own feet, undaunted by public opinion and pressure. The "Advertisement" (preface) of *Mary, A Fiction* makes claims of originality that only characters that have an element of autobiography are really convincing. She is doing something new in depicting a thinking woman. In it she declares *Mary, A Fiction* to be an "artless tale" that displays the "mind of a woman, who has thinking powers" (4). Tongue in cheek, Wollstonecraft "acknowledges" in a rare jesting moment that female organs cannot foster intellectual engagement, but wonders if an individual could at least *imagine* a thinking woman: "Without arguing physically about possibilities—in a fiction, such a being may be allowed to exist; whose grandeur is derived from the operation of its own faculties, not subjugated to opinion; but drawn by the individual from the original source."[9]

From the opening chapters in which she negatively describes Mary's mother as a "gentle, fashionable girl . . . educated with the expectation of a large fortune," who has become a "mere machine," Wollstonecraft explicates her fresh views on women. This "machine" image exposes both the objectification of women as commodities for the marriage market and their passive acceptance of male directive. Nonetheless, despite having chastity foisted upon her to placate society, Mary's mother compensates with vicarious pleasure from reading novels. (This view of chastity as an institutionalized demand marked a sharp break from the standard view of female sexual abstinence as an essential element in the basic moral framework of society. In the eighteenth century, virginity before marriage and chastity after it constituted a woman's most valued "possessions," without which a respectable woman could expect precious little from life—hence the numerous "fallen women" in novels of the era.[10] Wollstonecraft's view of chastity as a societally imposed phenomenon energetically defied this norm.)

In a sequence of clumsily shifting tones and scenarios, controversial views of women continue as Wollstonecraft depicts Mary's treatment at the hands of her mother: "When Mary the little blushing girl appeared she [mother] would send the awkward thing away.... Neglected in every respect, and left to the operations of her own mind, she considered everything that came under her inspection and learned to think" (9-10). Here, along with self-pity, blossoms an early intimation of the recurring debate between reason and feeling that concerned Wollstonecraft to the end of her life. A solitary, wandering, unloved Mary consciously trains herself to think rationally, deriving intellectual as well as emotional satisfaction from her devotion to sick, impoverished people and to animals: "She was miserable when beggars were driven from the gate without being relieved ... she would give them her own breakfast, and feel gratified, when, in consequence of it, she was pinched by hunger" (12-13). Denied the expression of tender feelings at home, Mary becomes the "creature of impulse, and the slave of compassion.... She denied herself every childish gratification, in order to relieve the necessities of the inhabitants [of the fisherman's huts]" (13, 18). It is meant to be a feeling picture of the growth of a philanthropist, and in part it is; but the longing for love that emerges shows how clearly philanthropy is a compensation for feeling, while extreme asceticism replaces the gratification Mary wishes.

Mary as Independent Heroine

Because Mary determinedly analyzes her own situation, she becomes more sharply aware of her spiritual impoverishment. Still, she prefers to serve the physical and spiritual needs of others because she is able to do so, and in her insecure state of mind a sense of accomplishment counts for something. She lets her mind guide her rather than rely on the advice of family or friends from whom a young woman would be expected to seek help. Nonetheless, her lack of any sophisticated knowledge of the world causes her capitulation to oversensuality or unrestrained passion, attractions that consign her to a life of intense emotionality. "It was the will of Providence," intones the omniscient narrator, "that Mary should experience almost every species of sorrow" (30).

Family and society decree it their responsibility to choose her future spouse, and indeed they successfully arrange her marriage to Charles so as to join two family estates. Mary turns her back on both, however, and pursues a comforting and comfortable (for a while) relationship with her friend, Ann (fictional embodiment of Fanny Blood). Although an isolated, unhappy Mary wants her friend to love her, Ann can only return gratitude for Mary's compassionate aid.

For her fiction, Mary Wollstonecraft has recast and transposed some facts of her relationship with Fanny Blood. Wollstonecraft's letters to George Blood about Hugh Skeys and her feelings after their marriage indicate that the reluctance of Ann of the story to return the fictional Mary's love might have been echoed in Wollstonecraft's life, insofar as Fanny Blood clearly hoped to wed Skeys. "If she had gone a year or two ago her health might have been perfectly restored," she confided to George in July 1785, ". . . How Hugh could let Fanny languish in England while he was throwing money away at Lisbon, is to me inexplicable if he had a passion that did not require the *fuel* of seeing the object—I much fear he loves her not for the qualities that render her dear to my heart."[11] Despite this quasi-rejection, Mary cherishes her feelings and her attachment, and is even willing for Ann's sake to suffer an enforced marriage. The death of Mary's brother leaves her an heiress at the age of seventeen. When she attempts to assist Ann financially, her father vetoes this decision, insisting instead that she marry Charles to combine and secure the family properties. Unlike Wollstonecraft, Mary accepts (she can scarcely protest) this denial of her rights, calmly embracing the Christian consolation that happiness must always elude mortals on earth. Again like Wollstonecraft, religion salves her, a psychological tonic for her personal and domestic difficulties.

Predictably, her marriage travels an unorthodox path, for Mary depends on her friendship with Ann, not her relationship with Charles, for emotional sustenance. The language of passion and joyful affection punctuates the uneven prose. After her friend's death, the problems of the living relationship are forgotten and Mary vows eternal love just as Wollstonecraft expressed undying affection for Fanny.[12] Devastated now, Mary finds a substitute in the equally grief-stricken but cryptic Scotsman, Henry ("It is only to my violin I tell the sorrows," 59).

An archangel of sensibility, but through illness deprived of any threatening sexuality, Henry develops Wollstonecraft's theme of the required balance between sensibility and intellect. No sooner do Henry's tender feelings (and his similarity to Ann) attract Mary than her self-reflecting (and religion-based) tendencies reaffirm themselves. "Every opinion was examined before it was adopted . . . these researches made her a christian from conviction. . . . They who imagine they can be religious without governing their tempers, or exercising benevolence in its most extensive sense, must certainly allow, that their religious duties are only practised from selfish principles. Subjectivity is even condemned in nuns. . . . [Wrapped up in themselves, the nuns only thought of inferior gratifications . . . while on the other hand, Ann's] death disturbed her reasoning faculties. . . . All was impenetrable gloom" (39, 49, 55, 56).

Mary unburdens her internal struggle to Henry at their parting: "My affections are involuntary—yet they can only be fixed by reflection, and when they are they make quite a part of my soul, are interwoven in it, animate my actions, and form my taste: certain qualities are calculated to call forth my sympathies, and make me all I am capable of being. The governing affection gives its stamp to the rest—because I am capable of loving one, I have that kind of charity to all my fellow-creatures which is not easily provoked. Milton has asserted, 'That earthly love is the scale by which to heavenly we may ascent'" (106-7). She goes on to excoriate a world that "is ever hostile and armed against the feeling heart" (68), while often calling on reason— "thou boasted guide" (86)—to assist her in her "internal tumult" (86). Wollstonecraft lays bare Mary's dilemma toward the end of the book: "One moment she was a heroine, half determined to bear whatever fate should inflict; the next, her mind would recoil—and tenderness possessed her whole soul" (96).

Similar to Emma Courtney's feelings for another Henry in Mary Hays's novel, Mary's feelings flout the general ethic of the times. Typically, however, and unlike Emma Courtney "she never told her love," since women who approached men tended to be viewed as prostitutes or coquettes. Despite nonconsummation, the love between them means that a relationship outside marriage of a socially acceptable married woman enters the contemporary novel; the ideological emphasis shifts away from the necessity and propriety of marriage as an institution to an open discussion of love: "I know I am dear to thee—and my affection for thee is twisted with every fiber of my heart" (166). However she affects the reader, Mary regards herself less as a conventional young religious woman of her time and more as an individual who can choose relationships on the basis of her feelings and not society's dictates—in the case of her first love she selects the woman of her choice, in the second, a man other than her spouse. That she chooses people who are dying, however, might suggest her incapacity for "relationships," owing to her sad childhood and to social pressures.

The Role of Work

Having exhausted her fortune to keep Ann alive, Mary decides she will work to survive. She "at last informed the family, that she had a reason for not living with her husband, which must some time remain a secret—they stared—Not live with him! How will you live then? This was a question she could not answer; she had only about eighty pounds remaining, of the money she took with her to Lisbon; when it was exhausted where could she get more? I will work, she cried, do anything rather than be a slave" (81-82).

Such a bold step by a heroine in 1788 duplicates the step Mary Wollstonecraft herself took in writing and submitting this very novel to Joseph Johnson as a means of earning a living.[13] Again, her "thinking powers are displayed" as she transcends the loss of her fortune with a reasoning courage and an intention to work, as earnestly as she had earlier worked for the destitute.

This plan to earn her own living despite social proscription also guarantees her maximum control over her life, contrary to the customary condition of women. Eighteenth-century women were "non-citizens who had no civil rights, who could not vote, own property, make wills, testify in court, serve on juries or obtain divorces, whose children belonged exclusively to the father, who could not even sign their names to checks or maintain bank accounts."[14] For Mary as for Wollstonecraft, this decision to live and work for economic independence (despite educational limitations) granted considerable liberation from an unjust balance of power within patriarchal society. Although the narrative never again mentions Mary's plan to work, let alone its implementation, that option still hovers: when marriages fail, alternatives are possible.

Conclusion

In the last fifty pages Mary once more seesaws between reason and feeling. Choosing a rational over an emotional approach, she has concealed her feelings from Henry. "Oh! reason," she exclaims, "why desert me, like the world, when I most need thy assistance!" (86). Henry's impending death finally makes possible open recognition of their love without the problem of physical consummation, a conveniently acceptable resolution.

The moribund Henry wants his mother to accept Mary as her offspring, almost as an offering to help comfort the older woman for his death. (Henry's loving mother contrasts starkly with Mary's socially conditioned mother, who resembles Lady Kingsborough, empty, fashionable, egocentric, and probably fiction-loving.) "My Mary," he entreats, "will you be comforted?" (107). In a tersely depicted but moving scenario, Wollstonecraft recasts a secular crucifixion with the women as heroes, in spite of the dying, always ethereal Henry. "It is dark; I cannot see thee; raise me. Where is Mary? . . . She heard distinctly the last sign—and lifting up to Heaven her eyes, Father, receive his spirit, she calmly cried" (107-108). Mary's passionate dedication to a man other than her husband solidifies her desire for a state—later she calls it "paradise"—in which no institution of marriage exists.

Had the book ended there, Mary would qualify as one of the new breed of women. Instead, from a sense of obligation and with "her disgust returned with additional force, in spite of previous reasonings" (110), she rejoins Charles. This hasty postlude underscores Mary's self-abnegation coupled with her hopes for an ultimate reunion with Henry. "She thought she was hastening to that world *where there is neither marrying* [italics Woll.], nor giving in marriage." In the light of Mary's initial devotion toward Ann ("Had Ann lived, it is probable she would never have loved Henry so fondly," 81), Mary's preference for Henry without any reference to her earlier love strikes an odd and even an inconsistent note unless the reader assumes that Mary has quite forgotten Ann. Most likely, Wollstonecraft's lack of literary experience explains the flaw.

Apart from Mary, the characters strike a wooden note; their emotions and actions are often unconvincing, and the story is written in a variable, choppy style. When she characterized *Mary, A Fiction* in later years as an "artless tale," dismissing it with contempt, Wollstonecraft acknowledged her literary naïveté. But the very fact that Mary elegizes an intimate female friend, writes a story about love between women in the first half, probes the tender-sweet sufferings of adolescence, makes political assertions about women's subjugation, reinforces the right of females to enter unorthodox relationships, and calls for increased confidence and autonomy among females along the way establishes the novel as an index to the age as well as to Wollstonecraft's developing ideas and sensibilities. It also proves how unformulated her notion of class was at this stage of her thinking. The concepts of charity and of leisured living remain uncriticized, but the need to aid the disadvantaged takes priority.

This first published novel contained elements that recur in Wollstonecraft's life and works: a pronounced tendency toward sentimentality, self-pity, disorienting shifts of time, and awkward language. The fictional Mary also resented the favoritism which her mother displayed toward her eldest son. One serious flaw (soon to be rectified) resided in Wollstonecraft's individualization of the problems of Mary and her mother, and of Ann and other characters. Wollstonecraft does not seem to "use" Mary as much as the later Maria, if at all, as a "type." Absorbed in herself and her career at this point, Wollstonecraft's insights remained subjective until new acquaintances and events and private thinking opened her vision to the need for collective political action and responsibility, for transcendence of particular individuals' problems.

In *Mary, A Fiction* Wollstonecraft infuses powerful, original ideas into the mind of an heroic female in a version of the sentimental novel that anticipates Romantic narrative art. She weaves themes of one woman's love for another woman with her love for a man who was not her spouse, then adds adultery of the mind and an attack on marriage, and champions the thinking woman who doubles as the separated wife. The style scarcely rises above the level of standard novels of the day, but its themes pinpoint a singular imagination and sensibility, the very act of writing an act of courage. Despite its shroud of conventional trappings, *Mary, A Fiction* is a startling if rudimentary manifesto of independent womanhood.

The Cave of Fancy

The Cave of Fancy, an unfinished philosophical tale (written also in 1787), remains Wollstonecraft's least successful work. Godwin rejoiced when she laid it aside.[15] Not only did she strive for embarrassing rhetorical flights, she sought to grasp a complex of situations and ideas beyond her reach. Her effort to fictionalize Johann Kasper Lavater's physiognomic theories probably rated as her most egregious error, as much for the oddity of the choice of subject as for the jaggedness of its execution.

Lavater insisted that "intellectual life, or the powers of the understanding and the mind, make themselves most apparent in the circumference and form of the solid parts of the head; especially the forehead."[16] If that were not strange enough, Wollstonecraft also ingested and popularized his reactionary views on women, summed up in his statement that "a woman with a beard is not so disgusting as a woman who acts the free thinker." She had almost expunged Lavater's ideas about the relationship between physiognomy and character from her writings by 1789, but her temporary attraction to these concepts was bound up with her attraction for Fuseli.[17] Lavater had dedicated his earlier work, *The Aphorisms of Men* (1787) to Fuseli, who translated and amplified it in 1789. Meanwhile, Thomas Holcroft and Wollstonecraft were separately translating Lavater's magnum opus *Physiognomie* from the German. This was a task she was undoubtedly relieved to abandon when Holcroft's edition was published, since her German, like her French, Italian, and Dutch, was rather painstakingly self-taught. Lavater's ideas must have generated discussion in the robust intellectual atmosphere of Johnson's circle, particularly with Fuseli there frequently and Lavater himself occasionally.

A literary pastiche, the fragmentary and thoroughly incomplete *The Cave of Fancy* defies classification. Often compared to *Rasselas* because of its unimaginative off-key repetition of Samuel Johnson's opening sentence, it borrows an overdone exotic setting and a clumsy framing device from the popular eighteenth-century oriental tale. The book reads as a rag-bag fragment that links other tag-ends and ideas: the shipwreck story (also popular in the eighteenth century), a crude, cropped educational manual promoting notions of rousseauist sensibility, autobiography as fiction, an abiding interest in females, and theories of physiognomy and hartleyan psychology.

The first two sketched-out chapters function as backdrop and introduction to a fictional treatise on female education that features a desert-island environment where a sage named Sagestus lives alone. One morning he finds a shipwreck with one survivor, a child crying for her mother. The sage drugs her to induce needed sleep.

In the second chapter, as Sagestus scrutinizes the dead around him, Wollstonecraft offers an abbreviated and facile disquisition on Lavater's physiognomic concepts. By having Sagestus deduce their characters physiognomically, she dismisses the dead sailors in a few paragraphs as a group seemingly unworthy of consideration: the first corpse, for example, has a "spacious forehead" where "warm fancy had revelled." The description of another huge corpse succinctly conveys the assumed relationship among physiognomy, character, and disposition: "A huge form was stretched near him, that exhibited marks of overgrown infancy; every part was relaxed; all appeared imperfect. Yet, some undulating lines on the puffed-out cheeks, displayed signs of timid, servile good nature; and the skin of the forehead had been so often drawn up in wonder, that the few hairs of the eyebrows were fixed in a sharp arch, whilst an ample chin rested in lobes of flesh on his protuberant breast" (115).

The child's mother, the only female in the wreck apart from the child herself, provokes thoughts as belittling as those applied to the sailors, consonant with Wollstonecraft's occasional impatience with women: "Men and women are all in their proper places—this female was intended to fold up linen and nurse the sick" (122-25). There follows a long, detailed portrait of the mother that concludes with the sage's conviction that "the orphan was not very unfortunate in having lost such a mother" (125). He decides to adopt the child, naming her Sagesta after himself.

This comment about the role of women introduces a disturbing dimension in Wollstonecraft's writing that also turns up in her later volume on the French Revolution, although its presence there is for more compelling personal reasons. That she would bow to Fuseli (or to Johnson) in translating a work by a man like Lavater who goes beyond even Rousseau in his offensive view of women remains puzzling. (Admittedly, however, she also praises Rousseau at this time.) "Among a thousand females," states Lavater, "there is scarcely one without the generic feminine signs; the flexible, the circular, and the irritable. They are the counterpart of man, taken out of man, to be subject to man; to comfort him like angels and to lighten his cares. . . . Men are most profound; women are more sublime" (400-401). He continues with countless axioms in this vein to demonstrate female inferiority. At one level, perhaps, her translation suggests the depth of her feeling for Fuseli as well as the transitional state of her own thinking. It might also prefigure her limited inability to discriminate under emotional stress. Yet when she had an excuse, Wollstonecraft set aside this misogynous work, probably recognizing the bankruptcy of Lavater's ideas as she became more confident of her own. In the passage describing Sagesta's mother she might have been exorcizing negative feelings about her dead mother while at the same time advocating the separate characters of the sexes, a notion she never completely abandoned. Her treatment of mothers in these early works of fiction and her harsh passages about Lady Kingsborough in *Original Stories* and about parental love in *Thoughts* strongly suggest that Wollstonecraft minded her mother's neglect very much and let it prey (unconsciously) on her mind. It even seems likely that it was partly because of this denied love, which bred her insecurity and anger, that she took to writing at all.

Purpose and Preoccupations

The last section of *The Cave of Fancy* provides the best clue to Wollstonecraft's purpose. It consists of "a variety of characters and stories presented to her [the orphan] in the Cave of Fancy" (2:126). A spirit narrates her history as the daughter of an oppressed, pitiable mother and a mercurial father. The virtue of active benevolence (charity) and the significance of heavenly as opposed to earthly love, compensations that gratify the spirit-narrator, punctuate the ending. Life here remarkably resembles Wollstonecraft's family life: the unhappy home, an unsatisfying marriage for the sake of her mother (quite possibly Eliza's marriage), an impossible love (Fanny Blood) who dies. The spirit also resembles Wollstonecraft when it "silently anticipated the happiness she should enjoy, when she entered those mansions, where death-divided friends should meet, to part no more" (2:139). The final metaphysical note, not dissimilar to the same final note in *Mary, A Fiction*, affirms the importance Wollstonecraft attached to religion in early education. Notably, her incapacity to render charity, leisure, marriage, and the lot of sailors within a clearly understood political context continues.

The spirit and the naïve child echo such earlier Wollstonecraft characters as Mary and Caroline in *Original Stories*, who also passively listened to the lessons being taught. Steeped in sensibility and voluptuous sorrow, which she later acknowledged as too earthly, the spirit chooses duty over love, but this absolute self-sacrifice engenders melancholy.

Although neither plot nor character has room to develop in this fragment, the story contains engaging aspects that confirm Wollstonecraft's current absorptions. The spirit-narrator marries from duty, yet retains a spiritual and passionate love for another beyond death. (Nowhere in her fiction does Wollstonecraft ever show a successful love relationship.) By the end, the spirit realizes that reason and judgment must prevail, and through them virtue and love of God. Price's ideas still predominate in an orthodox formation. Earthly love puts humanity in tune with a future heavenly state, provided that its virtuous essence remains intact. Thus humans unite with God. To have seen divinity in her lover's face not only proves the connection between pure earthly love and love for God, it forges the final link in the physiognomic chain. Just as brutes can have their essence physiognomically displayed, so God permits his own "likeness" in people of the highest virtue.

Similar platonic notions are scattered here and there but are never consistently pursued; possibly Thomas Taylor's influence hangs around as another vestigial philosophical strand.[18] The notion, too, of the "form"—of the cave and unsullied love—and the idea that people reflect divine essence remain undeveloped aspects of a sketchy platonic framework. (But the spirit continually reverses herself. When she realizes that she must be steadfast, she abandons earthly for spiritual preferences.)

The fragment reads as an inchoate attempt to depict crucial aspects of women's lives without much working knowledge of how to do so. The climax reads as a variation on the strong "I will work" statement of Mary in *Mary, A Fiction*, an ill-managed, overwritten, yet sensitive perception of how to persevere in times of despair. On the threshold of madness, the spirit thinks of Galileo, "who when he left the inquisition, looked upwards and cried out, 'Yet it moves.' " In agony she comprehends her will to continue, a dramatic moment and a dramatic scene recalling Wollstonecraft's early love of theater. "Yet I love," the spirit exclaims as she determines to endure (2:147).

The original plan for the book, which was to illustrate the process of female education in a series of informative (real-life rather than moralistic) stories seems to have been discontinued, for Wollstonecraft saw in time the unsuitability of the project. Nonetheless, as another revelation of her consuming interests at the time and of her developing style, *The Cave of Fancy* adds valuable information to the chart of Wollstonecraft's growth. Had she completed it, thoughts on the education of daughters would have repeated itself as a fundamental theme. After the spirit offers useful lessons and disappears, Sagestus indicates these priorities: "The senses of children should be the first object of improvement; then their passions worked on; and judgment the fruit" (2:131). Presumably, after pupils acquire reason, mentors can be dispensed with; like Mary and Caroline in *Original Stories*, they can become candidates for adult friendship.

William Godwin said of *The Cave of Fancy* in his memoirs: "She thought proper afterwards to lay [it] aside unfinished."[19] Consumed by a complex personal and political life, she did not return to fiction until her last years.

Chapter Four

A Vindication of
the Rights of Men

Wollstonecraft's *Vindication of the Rights of Men* was published in 1790. It answers Edmund Burke's *Reflections on the Revolution in France* and asserts Wollstonecraft's belief in liberty and political rights; it argues for greater equality for humanity and for the removal of traditional injustices of property and rank. The book is her first controversial work, her contribution to a literary war that raged in Britain from 1789 to the end of the century. It responds eloquently to her past experience and to the influence of the Dissenters and radicals, both wishing to reform the country and free oppressed groups from religious and social constraints. Joseph Johnson, who published *The Rights of Men*, did much to inspire it by the society he kept. Many political dinners at his house and many conversations with Fuseli must have preceded this polemical outburst.

Most particularly, it responds to the technical beginning of the French Revolution, the fall of the Bastille on July 14, 1789. To William Wordsworth, "bliss was it in that dawn to be alive," a sentiment shared by almost all people of liberal opinion in Britain. To Wollstonecraft the sudden upsurge of popular feeling was a political, ideological, and emotional event. It radicalized, inspired, and liberated her in a way no book or person could ever do. After the halting protests of *Mary, A Fiction* and *The Cave of Fancy*, she was suddenly ready to generalize and at last to transcend individual and personal problems.

Background

In November 1789, the Revolution Society, founded to commemorate the English Revolution of 1688, was addressed by Richard Price, Wollstonecraft's friend from the Newington Green days.[1] His

44

talk, entitled "A Discourse on the Love of Our Country," continued a debate begun the previous year over British political power and popular liberties; it was made controversial, however, by pointed reference to events in revolutionary France.[2]

Since the storming of the Bastille, the Assembly in France had adopted a resolution favoring the "rights of men," and in early October the Paris crowd had marched to Versailles and forcefully brought back the king and his family to the city. The action clearly affronted royal dignity and directly expressed the popular will. Price responded enthusiastically: "Thirty millions of people, indignant and resolute, spurning at slavery, and demanding liberty with an irresistible voice; their king led in triumph. And now methinks I see the ardour for liberty catching and spreading; a general amendment beginning in human affairs."[3]

Price claimed for the British no more than his Society had claimed the previous year, the rights of people to resist power when it was abused and to choose their rulers. In the context of French events, however, such claims seemed suddenly inflammatory and dangerous; this was the way that Edmund Burke, the Whig orator and apologist, understood them and he was outraged.[4] He countered Price's "Discourse" with an impassioned but closely reasoned address to the British, imploring them to understand the issues involved in the Revolution and to oppose its extension. *Reflections on the Revolution in France* was published a year after Price's work and went far beyond it in substance and length. Burke poured scorn on concepts of liberty and equality and argued against Price's belief in humanity's improvement and social progress. He advocated a conservative philosophy based on the wisdom of history; opposing the idea of perfectibility, he asserted the Christian humanist position, that humanity is indelibly flawed and that society is a fragile edifice, built in spite of rather than because of the essence of humanity. Those institutions, however imperfect, that have been proved by time—monarchy, hereditary honor and property, and class distinctions—should be cherished; without them humanity would reel back into brutishness, a fate he prophesied for revolutionary France.

Burke was horrified at the potential situation in France and feared it might poison Britain. He conveyed his alarm by describing the humiliation of the French royal family—a humiliation that suggested the breakdown in social order which Burke feared, as well as an end to respect for authority, which he believed held society together. His descriptions were powerfully emotional, using all the rhetorical devices of sentimental writing: pictures of attractive domesticity, appeals to the reader, and accounts of spontaneous feeling in the writer.

Reflections is an eloquent and persuasive plea for preserving the status quo, based on a belief that humanity is limited. The religious and political radicals of the day, however, opposed this belief and saw Burke's plea as one more weapon used by a corrupt ruling class to retain its position of privilege. Clearly an answer was necessary.

Wollstonecraft's Reply

From the beginning Wollstonecraft had followed the controversy between Price and Burke. In the *Analytical Review* of December 1789 she reviewed Price's "Discourse"; when Burke's *Reflections* appeared, she was one of its early readers. Fired by indignation at Burke's attack on radical ideas and especially at his abuse of Price, Wollstonecraft dashed off her *A Vindication of the Rights of Men*, one of the more than thirty replies to Burke. The most famous and substantial of these is Tom Paine's *Rights of Man*, but Wollstonecraft's work has the distinction of being the first. It was finished in less than a month after *Reflections* was published.

In her preface, Wollstonecraft states that she will confine herself to supporting the "grand principles" that Burke attacks (iv). By this she means that she will concentrate on her ideological differences with Burke, rather than on the immediate concerns of *Reflections*. Indeed she hardly mentions either the English Revolution or the French one, the immediate subjects for Burke and Price. Instead she declares her general views on political rights and liberty.

Against the conservative philosophy of Burke she urges her own experience mingled with ideas culled from Locke, Rousseau, and Price. Following Locke, who had so influenced her educational works, she defines human rights as "such a degree of liberty, civil and religious, as is compatible with the liberty of every other individual with whom he is united in a social compact, and the continued existence of that compact" (7-8). This liberty, she admits, has always been an ideal rather than a reality, for "the demon of property has ever been at hand to encroach on the sacred rights of men, and to fence around with awful pomp laws that war with justice" (8). These rights are not a modern revolutionary invention, not a burkean inheritance from history, not even a rousseauist condition of humanity; rather, they are "rights which men inherit at their birth, as rational creatures, who were raised above the brute creation by their improbable faculties." They receive them "not from their forefathers but from God" (22). These "rational rights" can never be undermined by prescription or by the traditions and institutions of the state, however venerable. ⅩIn Wollstonecraft's view, history is moving toward, not away from an ideal, and to conserve old principles and institutions is to hinder progressⅩ In the past, the strong gained riches through force, and through riches grew corrupt. Through hereditary property and honors the progress of civilization was stopped and the rights of humanity gave way to privilege for the upper class and charity for the lower. The customs and institutions of the past were established either through the "lawless power of an ambitious individual" or through the demands of "licentious barbarous insurgents" (13). In either case it was ludicrous to found on them the social organization of more enlightened ages. In Wollstonecraft's ringing words the constitution of England was made in the "dark days of ignorance, when the minds of men were shackled by the grossest prejudices and most immoral superstition"; if liberty were to be judged through such a past, it would be in a sorry state indeed: "Security of property! Behold, in a few words, the definition of English liberty" (19, 24).[5]

Much of Wollstonecraft's *Rights of Men* argues reasonably against the ideas of *Reflections*, but a large component of it criticizes and even abuses Burke. Certainly she seems to have forgotten Burke's own age when she flails him for his disrespect of the aging Price; for his sixty years Burke is rather taunted than revered.

Yet there is reason for the attack. Although William Godwin later blamed Wollstonecraft for her "contemptuous and intemperate" treatment of Burke, she herself held to the view of Pope and Johnson that literary faults stem from moral faults, that behind shallow writing is a shallow author. It was a view based on classical writings, especially of Quintilian, and it was put forward anew by Hugh Blair whose *Lectures on Rhetoric and Belles Lettres* she read in 1787. In Wollstonecraft's opinion, Burke who used pernicious rhetoric was pernicious himself and amply deserved the harshness she gave him. It was a view held also by Thomas Christie, her friend, who in *Letters on the Revolution in France . . . occasioned by the publication of the Right Hon.*

Edmund Burke (1791) claimed that Burke's "tuneful periods" were aimed at cheating the reader "into error and deception." The attack is open, fierce, and often cruel. In Wollstonecraft's pages Burke emerges as vain, trivial, and envious. Above all he is blamed for responding emotionally to events in a self-indulgent and yet calculating way. Burke, she argues, cries because he enjoys crying and because he knows the powerful influence of tearful prose. It is an interesting criticism from the author of the lachrymose *Mary, A Fiction.*

For Wollstonecraft, Burke's shallow emotionalism is displayed most clearly in his outpourings over high-placed misery and his silence over the wretchedness of the poor, whose sufferings reasonably deserve pity: "Misery, to reach your heart, I perceive, must have its cap and bells" (27), she taunts him. The same emotionalism, in Wollstonecraft's view, leads Burke to appreciate not the essence of religion but merely its institutional trappings; hence he laments the loss of church property, which she views as an aid to true religion. The callowness of Burke's answer in these cases springs from a lack of the fixed principles of reason, which alone in her opinion can provide right judgment and lead to an appropriate response.

The charge that Burke courts popularity at the expense of principle is reiterated throughout *The Rights of Men.* It is supported by the inconsistency Wollstonecraft finds between his past and present actions and opinions. Burke's opposition to the French Revolution, after his support of the North American one, becomes not a courageous following of conscience but a proof of his overwhelming desire for renown. He opposes for the sake of opposing and so that he might regain the fame lost in recent years. According to Wollstonecraft, such a man would have been a violent revolutionary if born a Frenchman, since he would always have pushed himself to the extremes where he could be noticed.

Wollstonecraft finds Burke's love of fame and his facile emotionalism combined in his manner of treating British and French royalty. The romantic gallantry shown the French king and queen is nowhere apparent when he deals with the British George III. Because the king opposes the Whigs, self-interest and party zeal cause Burke to make "insensible and profane" attacks on a man stricken with madness who deserves pity rather than censure (61). Bitterly she recalls Burke's powerful words to Parliament in 1789 during the Regency debate: "Did they recollect that they were talking of a sick king, of a monarch smitten by the hand of Omnipotence, and that the Almighty had hurled him from his throne. . . ."[6] Such vindictiveness toward a mentally sick man, she feels, justifies her own cruelty.

Wollstonecraft's Ideas

In *The Rights of Men,* Wollstonecraft moves easily from subject to subject and in passing alludes to a variety of ideas and philosophical controversies. She repeats her main points and constantly returns to topics with which the reader supposed she had finished. Such a repetitive and digressive method has value both in her earlier pedagogical manuals and in her later work, *A Vindication of the Rights of Woman.* In these works she is dealing with widely held prejudices and opinions that she wishes to keep always before the reader while expressing her positive views. In *The Rights of Men,* written to refute a single work, it detracts from the power of many of her points. Yet the digressive method has some justification from the standpoint of the lockean and hartleyan association of ideas she had espoused in her educational works, since it joins abstract concepts with entertaining concrete examples and so renders them memorable. This method also has some advantage for later readers; with it she covers a wide range of topics not always pertinent to the argument against Burke but always revealing about her own beliefs and concerns. In the digressions as well as in the main arguments she again shows her debt to her associates in the Johnson and Price circles and her ability to weld their ideas to her own experience.

As in her early pedagogical works, religion and morality remain extremely important to her, and she clearly states the opinions she has come to hold by 1790. As earlier, she retains a firm belief in a benevolent God, but she has moved further toward rejecting the doctrines of orthodox Christianity. She had never been much concerned with Christ and vicarious salvation; now she seems to ignore both.

Wollstonecraft's conception of God is conditioned by her overwhelming belief in reason. God is to be worshipped not because he demands it and because great power should be revered, but because he is the summation of reason: "I FEAR God! I bend with awful reverence when I enquire on what my fear is built.—I fear that sublime power, whose motive for creating me must have been wise and good; and I submit to the moral laws which my reason deduces from

this view of my dependence on him.—It is not his power that I fear—
it is not to an arbitrary will, but to unerring *reason* I submit" (16).

Wollstonecraft has no patience with the idea of innate depravity
and implied human limitations that were the foundation of Burke's
argument; she asserts that "children are born ignorant, consequantly
[sic] innocent" (72). She also rejects the belief that humanity has
introduced evil into the divine scheme, a concept newly put forward,
if in different guise, by social philosophers for example, who felt that
all evils were the result of improper education and social organization.
At this stage she is convinced that "both physical and moral evil were
not only foreseen, but entered into the scheme of Providence, when
this world was contemplated in the Divine mind" and that "there is
much unavoidable wretchedness, appointed by the grand Disposer of
all events" (133-34).

Although she had not always opposed the idea of innate moral
sense, Wollstonecraft does so firmly in *The Rights of Men* and she
quotes Burke contemptuously: "In England we have not yet been
completely emboweled of our natural entrails; we still feel within
us, and we cherish and cultivate those inbred sentiments which are the
faithful guardians, the active monitors of our duty, the true supporters
of all liberal and manly morals" (73-74). Burke's view makes reason
into a weak component of humanity, since it is frequently overwhelmed by the stronger emotions. To retain some belief in a moral
order in the face of this situation, he must necessarily separate reason
from the moral faculty. This pessimistic dualism Wollstonecraft now
utterly deplores.

In opposition to the idea of an instinctive morality, Wollstonecraft
offers the concept of Price that morality and reason are one.[7] Moral
truths are neither unknown nor instinctive but are within the sphere
of reason. Through reason a person may apprehend and follow the
virtuous way. Price's conception of reason and morality implies an optimistic view of humanity and its relationship with the creator, whose
reason in small measure it shares.

For organized and established religion, Wollstonecraft has a Dissenting scorn, although she was herself still nominally a member of
the Church of England. She attacks the established church for the
materialism and greed of its followers, especially the clergy. She scoffs
at the practice of providing a living for younger sons: "It is a well-
known fact, that when *we*, the people of England, have a son whom

we scarcely know what to do with," she writes sarcastically, "*we* make a clergyman of him" (17). With such a practice it is no wonder that the clergy are motivated by greed rather than piety and that they "perform the duty of their profession as a kind of fee-simple to entitle them to the emoluments accruing from it" (p. 86). Her contempt also envelops the absentee clergy, who do not even disguise their greed, and the clergyman tutors, who become living examples of the relationship between church and ruling class. In this, both sides are corrupted, for the aristocratic young man learns to despise the church, whose representative he dominates, and the clerical tutor degrades himself through this inappropriate submission to rank (90-91). In short, the Church of England is proof of Wollstonecraft's opinion, influenced by Price, that church and state should be separated and that religion and ethics should not. Without reason, which should be the basis of religion and ethics, the rituals of the Church of England are empty, and morality stands aloof from "this national religion, this ideal consecration of a state" (83).

To an even greater extent than her religious ideas, Wollstonecraft's political and social theories are culled from her experience and sharpened and articulated through her association with Dissenting and radical thinkers. She reacts to Burke's insistence on submission to authority with all the hatred she felt toward autocrats throughout her life; in yet another act of revenge on the Kingsboroughs she rails against the elite by birth, and castigates her own father when she criticizes unnatural and delinquent parents.

According to her reading of Burke, he advocated that the lower classes unquestionably submit to the state and to the aristocracy. This seemed pernicious doctrine to Wollstonecraft, who was well aware of the disastrous effects of such submission on both the giver and the receiver. To refute the doctrine, she describes in detail the effects of absolute subordination on the lower and upper classes and ridicules those institutions for which Burke demanded reverence.

Burke considered that the English Parliament was formed "under the auspices, and was confirmed by the sanctions of religion and piety"; it was worthy of the highest respect (80). Wollstonecraft, however, sees it as a contemptible body, exemplifying the worst in English society. Its past and present are, in her view, equally miserable; it was formed "as Europe was emerging out of barbarism" and in her time it consists of "the profligates of rank, emasculated by hereditary effeminacy" (80, 97). Elections to Parliament are farcical, for "sordid interest, or licentious thoughtlessness, is the spring of action." Through such descriptions she suggests respect for the English Parliament is as ridiculous as it is degrading.

Wollstonecraft reserves her harshest criticism for Burke's support of aristocracy and class distinctions. One of his arguments in favor of a nobility was that good birth gives awareness of illustrious ancestors and so dignifies character and conduct. Wollstonecraft scorns this idea and asserts that, on the contrary, high birth gives a "factitious pride that disemboweled the man" (103). Frequently, persons of high birth are of less merit than those of low, for they are marred by the bad effects of opulence and unmerited distinction. Unfortunately, too, the pernicious results of rank are not confined to the class possessing it: the existence of an hereditary aristocracy robs the lower class of proper pride and self-respect and the middle class of identity, for its members vie with each other in aping the faults of the social class they envy. The canker of privilege affects the fortunate and the unfortunate alike, for "the respect paid to rank and fortune damps every generous purpose of the soul, and stifles the natural affections on which human contentment ought to be built" (52).

In Wollstonecraft's view, the great instrument of class distinction and social oppression is inheritance. This institution takes away the incentive of both rich and poor, and makes a mockery of genius and merit. It also distorts the relationship that should exist between parents and children, as she herself had experienced long before she came to formulate her idea. Parents make slaves of their children through their financial power, and sacrifice younger children for the sake of the eldest son, who is to inherit "what was called, with shameful falsehood, the *family* estate"—a misnomer she attacked again in *The Wrongs of Woman*. On their side, children return hatred, desiring their parents' death as the only means of obtaining riches they have neither earned nor deserved (46).

In spite of the obvious rancor that inspires her attack, Wollstonecraft's solution to the social enormity is not extreme. In the ideal society she envisages, she would presumably destroy inherited honors, but inherited property would in part remain: "the only security of property that nature authorizes and reason sanctions is, the right a man has to enjoy the acquisitions which his talents and industry have acquired; and to bequeath them to whom he chooses" (51). From other passages it is clear that she does not include huge properties in this statement, for she wants large estates such as the Kingsboroughs' to be carved into small farms and distributed to the peasants. Her ideal is then a society not of huge private holdings or indeed of communal ones, but of small private businesses and farms such as she later found in Norway. This ideal is in keeping with the importance she places on individualism and liberty, so far as they allow the proper degree of social equality. Clearly, she is here in the broad stream of British liberal thought and allied with the moderate girondists in France, and even to some extent with the jacobins who, although more prepared than their rivals to embrace the idea of a directed economy held by some working class revolutionary groups, nonetheless supported property rights and a controlled private enterprise.

In *The Rights of Men* Wollstonecraft thinks of the subordinate class primarily in terms of men. Many years will have to pass before she sees her own sex as a coherent group within the class or as a group that crosses class lines, united by a particular oppression. Indeed, she is still trapped by language in such a way that she sees men as the norm and women as the deviant, and she still terms the ultimate weakness "effeminacy" and social corruption "emasculation." Yet throughout her writing life, from *Thoughts* onward she has been disturbed by women's state and it would be surprising if it were not a topic in her first overtly political work. She had seen Burke fawning on the feminine delicacy of Marie Antoinette in *Reflections*, a woman who in Wollstonecraft's prose becomes rather like the "mere machine," Mary's mother in *Mary, A Fiction*. In the *Philosophical Enquiry into the Sublime and Beautiful* she had earlier read his opinion that "The beauty of women is considerably owing to their weakness or delicacy, and is even enhanced by their timidity, a quality of mind analogous to it."[8] Such antifeminist opinions appalled her as thoroughly as Burke's indifference to the lower class, and she made a combined attack on both in a section on aristocratic women. Although she clearly had to refine and develop her thinking before beginning *The Rights of Woman*, she has in this section all the ideological components of her later work.

In *The Rights of Men*, Wollstonecraft argues that females of the upper class are only half human. For them flirtation has become the "grand business of life," and their whole concern must be to please men; they can thus be defined entirely as sexual beings (48). Such exclusive concern confines their understanding and makes them weak and contemptible. Wollstonecraft feels deeply that life should be a serious business, a preparation for eternity, and should not be degraded into a trivial pursuit of pleasure. Since women have souls, they should cultivate moral virtue, which alone has eternal beauty, and not the transient sexual beauty demanded of them by society. This argument has emerged from her later educational works; expanded with illustration and analysis, it becomes the primary message of *The Rights of Woman*.

Style

"I glow with indignation," Wollstonecraft exclaims in *The Rights of Men* (9). The sentence could be the motto of her work. The indignation, together with the method of publication—Johnson had each section set in type while she wrote the next—explains something of the stylistic excess and organizational defects of this first polemic. In addition, its unity cannot have been helped when, halfway through, Wollstonecraft lost confidence in herself and announced to Johnson that she could not proceed. His astute handling of the situation—he accepted her decision, offering to destroy what he had already typeset—propelled her into the second part of the work.

But none of these factors explains everything, for the digressive habits and the metaphorical language are characteristics of all her writings, and in her revision for the second edition she did not omit digressions for the sake of the clarity of the whole. Outbursts of rhetoric are indiscriminately scattered throughout her books, and frequently she fails to integrate her stylistic riches into the surrounding prose.

Notwithstanding her own uneven and emotional style, early in *The Rights of Men* Wollstonecraft takes pains to establish herself as an author associated with reason, honest indignation, and "manliness." The purpose of this is to distinguish her declarations of wrath from those of Burke and give them the substance she considers his lack. Another is to associate Burke, the antagonist, with weak sensibility, unnecessary compassion, and ironically "effeminacy."

Toward the beginning of *The Rights of Men* she mentions Burke's "theatrical attitudes" and "sentimental exclamation," suitable for "the

Ladies," and contrasts them with the just arguments of herself, the "dry reasoner" (5). Throughout the work she repeats objections to Burke's style, seen as the outward manifestation of his inner weakness. In the Advertisement, for example, he is a "desultory writer" whose "devious tracks" the "reasoner" has "no patience to follow" (iv). Elsewhere his utterances are described as "turgid bombast" (65).

In opposition, the "reasoner" flaunts her stylistic limitations and plainness: "I have not yet learned to twist my periods," she proudly asserts, "nor, in the equivocal idiom of politeness, to disguise my sentiments, and imply what I should be afraid to utter" (1). She insists she will not "condescend to cull" her words (2).

Yet, if Wollstonecraft succeeds in showing she is moved by honest and not counterfeit indignation, she fails to associate herself with a rationalism that excludes emotion. In fact, she uses the "manie for sensibility," or excessive emotionalism, to her own end as surely and often as skillfully as Burke, for like him she knows that polemic must win the heart and so take the mind by storm. Her rhapsody on Price is certainly as emotionally rhetorical as Burke's on the French queen, and its purpose is similar: "I could almost fancy that I now see this respectable old man, in his pulpit, with hands clasped, and eyes devoutly fixed, praying with all the simple energy of unaffected piety; or, when more erect, inculcating the dignity of virtue, and enforcing the doctrines his life adorns; benevolence animated each feature, and persuasion attuned his accents; the preacher grew eloquent, who only laboured to be clear; and the respect that he extorted, seemed only the respect due to personified virtue and matured wisdom.—Is this the man you brand with so many opprobrious epithets? he whose private life will stand the test of the strictest enquiry—away with such unmanly sarcasms, and puerile conceits" (35-36).

Other declamatory peaks are equally effective, while they avoid the element of bathos in the passage on Price. Considering Burke's shallow response to the Revolution, for example, she exclaims: "Man preys on man; and you mourn for the idle tapestry that decorated a gothic pile, and the dronish bell that summoned the fat priest to prayer" (152). Without ever having orated in Parliament or declaimed from the pulpit, she has here captured the intonation of impassioned public speech. Perhaps her careful reading of *The Speaker* and her compilation of *The Female Reader* gave her the experience imaginatively.

Many of Wollstonecraft's most highly charged passages are direct addresses to Burke, a fact that considerably weakens her claim to dry reason but increases the power and point of her attack. "Observe, Sir, that I called your piety affectation," she thunders, "a rant to enable you to point your venemous dart, and round your periods. I speak with warmth, because, of all hypocrites, my soul most indignantly spurns a religious one" (55-56).

Elsewhere she intimates a nefariousness in Burke that she will not even describe. Her own suggestion rouses her to an indignation that seems to owe little to the justice she advocates for the polemical writer: "But to return from a digression which you will more perfectly understand than any of my readers—on what principle you, Sir, can justify the reformation, which tore up by the roots an old establishment, I cannot guess—but I beg your pardon, perhaps you do not wish to justify it—and have some mental reservation to excuse you, to yourself, for not openly avowing your reverence. Or, to go further back;—had you been a Jew—you would have joined in the cry, crucify him!—crucify him!" (21). It is certainly difficult to reconcile such an attack with the character of the "just reasoner."

Undoubtedly, many criticisms can be leveled at Wollstonecraft's style and emotional excess in *The Rights of Men*. Yet both combine to distinguish her writing and express her personality. In contemporary reviews, a line flashes out from the page, immediately proclaiming its author and the spirit in which she wrote.[9] If her aim is to jolt the reader into thinking about rather than accepting her ideas, style is well suited to purpose.

Autobiographical Elements

The personal abuse of Burke, the rhetorical flights, and the impulsive digressions all indicate that Wollstonecraft is fully engaged and is fighting more than an intellectual battle in her book. Indeed she refers to her own experiences throughout the work, and hints that she is in a way vindicating her life as well as general political rights. If Burke were correct in his demand that authority be reverenced for the sake of social order, she would surely be culpable on many counts, social and religious, as well as political.

Wollstonecraft's resentment against her eldest brother clearly leaps from *The Rights of Men*, even though in the second edition she changes from the first to the third person in passages (possibly) dealing with her family life. Burke supported primogeniture as one of the pillars of social order. Wollstonecraft, who argues that no individual should be sacrificed to some imaginary good of society as a whole, infuses her argument against Burke with all the bitterness she felt about the sacrifice of herself and the younger children to the welfare of the eldest son (46), "a being privileged by nature," she bitterly wrote later in *The Wrongs of Woman*.

When Wollstonecraft criticizes Burke's view of religion as a ritual communality of worship, she again uses her private experience. After the death of Fanny Blood, she had found great consolation in inward religion. If Burke's socially oriented view of religion is correct, she has been merely self-indulgent in her action and belief.

A more conjectural example of Wollstonecraft's including personal experience in her argument derives from Emily Sunstein's idea that her younger brother, Henry, who disappeared from the family records, went insane and was confined in an asylum.[10] If the idea is correct, it explains Wollstonecraft's bitterness and indignation at Burke's treatment of the mad George III, for she would have known at first hand the true misery of insanity. Not usually a supporter of kings, she lets forth an invective against Burke for his treatment of George III that takes her for the moment far from the subject of political rights. In the process she reveals a horror of madness with which she may well have been haunted in her life:

A father torn from his children,—a husband from an affectionate wife,— a man from himself! ... The sight of august ruins, of a depopulated country—what are they to a disordered soul! when all the faculties are mixed in wild confusion. It is then indeed we tremble for humanity— and, if some wild fancy chance to cross the brain, we fearfully start, and pressing our hand against our brow, ask if we are yet men?—if our reason is undisturbed?—if judgment hold the helm. ... Had not vanity or interest steeled your heart, you would have been shocked at the cold insensibility which could carry a man to those dreadful mansions, where human weakness appears in its most awful form to *calculate* the chances against the King's recovery. Impressed as *you are* with respect for royalty, I am astonished that you did not tremble at every step, lest Heaven should avenge on your guilty head the insult offered to its vicegerent. But the conscience that is under the direction of transient ebullitions of feeling, is not very tender or consistent, when the current runs another way. (58, 62)

This passage seems at first sight a digression from Wollstonecraft's main argument against subordination, so antipathetic to her philosophy and experience; yet in one way it reinforces it. Throughout *The Rights of Men* she asserts that unreasoned respect for and subservience to any person or institution whatsoever is degrading and destructive of deep feeling. In Burke's treatment of the mad king, he reveals a character that has been affected by the attitude of subordination. A conscience that was synonymous with reason rather than instinct would not have allowed such a misjudgment and such an immoral response.

Wollstonecraft argues that the canker of subordination has eaten into all classes of society; this apprehension has come from her life's bitter experience as well as from her philosophy. The more effective passages reveal this experience, the character that has been formed by it, and the philosophy that has by this time come to explain it:

Surveying civilized life, and seeing, with undazzled eye, the polished vices of the rich, their insincerity, want of natural affections, with all the specious train that luxury introduces, I have turned impatiently to the poor, to look for man undebauched by riches or power—but, alas! what did I see? a being scarcely above the brutes, over which he tyrannized; a broken spirit, worn-out body, and all those gross vices which the example of the rich, rudely copied, could produce. Envy built a wall of separation, that made the poor hate, whilst they bent to their superiors; who, on their part, stepped aside to avoid the loathsome sight of human misery.

What were the outrages of a day [the march to Versailles] to these continual miseries? Let those sorrows hide their diminished head before the tremendous mountain of woe that thus defaces our globe! (151-52)

It is a powerful passage, in which the first-person pronoun is admirably integrated. Effective in itself, it draws a moving portrait of Wollstonecraft the polemicist, which, despite the contempt of reviewers who ridiculed a woman's asserting the rights of "man,"[11] is one of the glories of the book.

Chapter Five

A Vindication of the Rights of Woman

In *A Vindication of the Rights of Woman* Wollstonecraft extends the arguments of *The Rights of Men* to cover the group of humanity excluded from the supposedly generic "man." The work is the culmination of her experience as a woman, as a polemical author, and as a member of the radical intellectual groups of Price and Johnson. Like her early works, it is pedagogical, but it goes beyond them in its insistence on intellectual, emotional, and physical development for women. It is a revolutionary demand that attacks both male dominance and female acquiescence. Ironically, however, its ringing lines were composed when she herself was victim of the excessive sensibility she condemned, a prey to an infatuation encouraged by her female education but forbidden by society. Her love of Fuseli may in time have led her to understand women's needs more deeply, but at first it served mainly to illustrate the female predicament she deplored. The book, then, speaks from and to its author's experience.

The British Background

The Rights of Woman responds to a literary tradition and to a changing social climate. Wollstonecraft does not mention the authors of the late seventeenth and early eighteenth centuries who wrote constructively about women's condition even if they did not anticipate her radical proposals. She does, however, mention and quote those who epitomize the tradition long dominant in English literature of denigrating women, possibly because these writers were better known and possibly because she wished to stress her own originality. Writers in this misogynist tradition usually both condemned women's frailty and archly praised it. Wollstonecraft is not amused at the sprightly satire of Pope and Swift, and she quotes with distaste from "To a

Lady: Of the Characters of Women" in which women are termed
"fine by defect." Her attitude is the same when she contemplates the
unsatirical view held by one of her own sex of women as half-beings;
Anna Laetitia Barbauld, so much admired in other areas, asserted that
women were born "for pleasure and delight alone."[1]

In Wollstonecraft's day, various factors had modified the harsh literary view of women. The first was the abundance of female novelists
like Fanny Burney, Charlotte Smith, Clara Reeve, and Elizabeth Inchbald, who presented heroines of moral if not always intellectual stature. Some of these novelists Wollstonecraft had reviewed for the
Analytical Review, and she had been lavish in her praise whenever
she discovered anything close to a satisfactory portrait of a woman.

A second factor was the growth of humanitarian and enlightened
sentiment that drew attention to the poor, the weak, and the despised;
all three categories included women. Wollstonecraft attacked this
humanitarian sentiment in Burke when she believed it misdirected,
but her own rhapsody on Price when she felt him misused reveals
that she was not immune to its influence. Translated into the literary
mode, humanitarianism became sentimentalism, a literary movement
that made a heady combination of virtue and emotion. Sentimental
pictures taught and moved, to tears if possible; they appealed especially to female readers, constantly told of their association with the
heart, and they often included women in various postures of distress.
In *The Rights of Woman* Wollstonecraft regards "with sympathetic
emotion" her own picture of the mother of modest means surrounded
with "smiling babes"; later she recollects "with pleasure" the pupil
of a country day school returning "to recount the feats of the day
close at the parental knee." In both passages the emotive effect comes
from an extreme contrast with a vicious aristocratic system described
immediately before. The effective humanitarian passage, whether on
mothers, abused animals, or French queens, also relies on such sensational contrasts.

A third factor was the existence of the Bluestockings. This group
of women, which included Hannah More, Elizabeth Carter, Elizabeth
Montagu, and Hester Chapone, gained some position in a male world
through combining piety, seriousness, and learning. But they wanted
this position neither improved for themselves nor extended to others;
Hannah More, for example, desired changes in the conduct rather than
in the subordinate position of women, which she regarded as divinely

appointed. Similar to Wollstonecraft in her emphasis on religion, she would have rejected Wollstonecraft's rationalist belief in the perfectibility of humanity on earth. Unfortunately, we have no specific comments from More on *The Rights of Woman*, for she refused to read the book, dismissing it as "metaphysical jargon." After Wollstonecraft's death she attacked the "presumptuous vanity dishonorable to their sex" of those "female pretenders" who advocated women's rights.[2]

Certainly the Bluestockings were not radical in their desires for women; yet through their intellectual and social stature, as well as their literary works, they helped form a tolerant climate of opinion concerning women. *The Rights of Woman* was thus received more favorably than it would have been earlier in the century or than it was in the next.

The major Bluestockings had little immediate influence on Wollstonecraft however, in fact, she seems to have read very few of the earlier women writers on her sex, radical or conservative. The exception of course is Catherine Macaulay, enthusiastically reviewed in the *Analytical Review* and acknowledged in Wollstonecraft's text. Because of this accepted influence and because Macaulay's *Letters on Education* anticipate *The Rights of Woman* in so many respects, it is worth glancing at the two authors together.

In all essential ideas on women Wollstonecraft and Macaulay agree politics, religion, and pedagogy. Both feel that the tyranny of men harms the mind and character of women, just as the tyranny of government scars a people. Both stress the value of learning for girls, believing that it contributes to rather than destroys piety and virtue. Like Locke, so important an influence on Wollstonecraft's early educational works, the two connect moral and intellectual education. They vigorously support coeducation on the grounds that separating the sexes during school years leads to a false peculiarly female standard for women. Again, both follow Locke in advocating outdoor physical exercise for girls and deplore the affected and pitiful image of frail women presented by male writers such as Burke and Rousseau. Wollstonecraft and Macaulay are also in accord when they contemptuously dismiss female accomplishments designed solely to render women sexually attractive, and they lash out against the harem mentality that allows this exclusive cultivation of the trivial. For each author, virtue is asexual and should be cultivated by men and women alike. They see the regeneration of society dependent on its treatment of women, and they believe together that women will take subtly and viciously what is not given to them as their right. They inveigh against women's status of civil nonentity and object to the practice of calling an inquiring female mind "masculine."

These are only a few of the ways in which Wollstonecraft and Macaulay agree in opinion and argument, and even a cursory reading of the *Letters on Education* will reveal many other striking similarities.[3] The differences of opinion mentioned in the review and confirmed by *The Rights of Woman* are slight, yet worth noting. Wollstonecraft emerges as more of a pragmatist in education and rationalist in religious matters than Macaulay, who depends for belief entirely on revelation. In her review she finds Macaulay's exacting reading list for the young rather optimistic, and she stresses that the prejudice concerning female chastity should be weakened only when women have been educated sufficiently to base virtue on rational principles. When Macaulay considers that "*Example should* coincide with instruction," Wollstonecraft wryly exclaims: "True, O moralist!—But then thou shouldst educate two generations."

The main distinction between the two authors, however, is in form and style, not opinion. Far more than Macaulay, Wollstonecraft attacks the vices of women as they are, drawing from experience devastating pictures of contemporary women of the idle aristocracy and ignorant bourgeoisie. She is on the whole more forceful and audacious than her predecessor and it was in the energy of her expression that she was judged by reviewers to be most shocking.

The French Background

In revolutionary France, the country from which so much support might have been expected, Wollstonecraft had little precedent for her feminist views The philosophers of the Enlightenment held orthodox ideas of women as weaker vessels and adjuncts of men, although they shared Wollstonecraft's belief that education can improve humanity.

Having destroyed most of the educational system of the old regime, the French revolutionaries tried to replace it with one more suitable for a new democratic and secular society. The preamble to the Constitution of 1791 stated that all institutions "which were injurious to liberty and equality of rights" and all "privilege" had been abolished.

Title I of the Constitution put this positively regarding education in its proposal of "public instruction for all citizens."

The rights of men, including their right to education, clearly preoccupied the revolutionaries; only a minority of thinkers considered extending these rights to women. In the early years of the Revolution, some women exclaimed in pamphlets and petitions to the Assembly at the many peculiar grievances of their sex. They demanded, for example, that men be excluded from certain jobs so that women would have the right to work and would not be forced into idleness and prostitution. They asked for female education, civil rights for spinsters and widows, and reform of marriage laws seen as particularly harsh on women. One feminist journal even suggested women should be represented in the Assembly and that they should have sexual freedom equivalent to men's. Women established clubs in which they announced their demands and fashioned their ideas on equality. Yet although they occasionally appeared as a militant and separate force, these women almost always subordinated their demands to wider human considerations and their own good to the revolutionary society of which they were a part. Thus no single adequate document of any length came out of the Revolution to express the unique feminist position and desires.

The French works that most closely anticipated *The Rights of Woman* were by the Marquis de Condorcet and Olympe de Gouges. Both authors demanded improved education for women in addition to concerning themselves with political and economic rights. Olympe de Gouges based her feminist ideas on the *Declaration of the Rights of Man*, recently placed as preface to the Constitution of 1791. Although its proposals had seemed so universal in their application, she showed how women were excluded from them, how privilege had been retained for men, and equality denied to women. She advocated extending men's rights to women. Many of her ideas were similar to Wollstonecraft's, but less insistently expressed and less realized by example.[4]

In *Letters to a Citizen of New-Haven* (1788) and *On the Admission of Women to the Suffrage* (1790) Condorcet proposed full educational rights for women.[5] His proposal was taken up but vastly modified by Talleyrand, who presented his *Report on Public Instruction* in September 1791.[6] This plan was designed to fulfill the require-

ments of education in Title I of the Constitution, and it bore out
Gouges' statement that women were not included in the general rights,
for it made hardly any provision for their education. According to
the plan, girls were to be educated with boys until the age of eight;
thereafter they were to remain at home in domestic employment.

Much of Talleyrand's report was rejected by the committee set up
to bring about a national education, and in April 1792 Condorcet in
his *Report on Education* reiterated the importance of female education.[7] He did not suggest coeducation at the primary school level
except where a town was too small to support two schools, and he
failed to deal with women's more advanced education, promising to
devote another report to their training in general. He did provide
a practical reason for the education of women that was similar to
Wollstonecraft's: women were the principal trainers of children in
the home, and many families were headed by widows.

According to a letter written in February 1793, Wollstonecraft
herself was working at that time on a plan of education for the French
committee on education.[8] There is no record that she completed or
presented this interesting document, but she would no doubt have
gone beyond Condorcet in arguing for coeducation at all levels and
for a syllabus as broad for girls as for boys.

When she was working on *The Rights of Woman* in 1791, Wollstonecraft was probably unacquainted with Olympe de Gouges, Condorcet, or any other French feminist writers. She knew, however, of
Talleyrand's *Report* and the importance of its author, and its official
nature must have suggested to her how little the French Revolution
was truly affecting the subordinate status of women. To change this
situation by influencing Talleyrand was the immediate, stated aim of
The Rights of Woman.[9] There is, however, no evidence that it
succeeded in this or affected by any other means the pedagogy of the
Revolution.

The Argument with Rousseau

As *The Rights of Men* responds to Burke's *Reflections*, so *The
Rights of Woman* in great part responds to Rousseau's *Emile* with
whose general ideas on education she seemed so much in agreement
when writing *Original Stories*, despite her need to change the gender

of the pupils.[10] Wollstonecraft had a larger polemical aim than to refute a single author, but certainly much of her argument arose from her scorn of Sophie, whom Rousseau held up as exemplary for womankind. Wollstonecraft had, however, learned much from Rousseau and she greatly admired his humanitarianism and liberal sympathy. Certainly in his opposition to tyranny and orthodoxy he was her guide and model, and in a letter to Imlay she later admitted, "I have always been half in love with him."[11] Perhaps, then, the fierceness of her attack on his view of women derived from her deep sympathy with his character and with his other ideas; she was angry that a man so admirable should now seem to be so far astray.

Wollstonecraft quotes Rousseau at length in her book, expressing her outrage at his opinion of women as totally subordinate to men and at his educational scheme that would fit females only for such a role. She emphasizes virtue and reason throughout in an attempt to correct Rousseau's view that young women need only cultivate those qualities that make them alluring to men.

In the early pages of *The Rights of Woman* Rousseau is already one of those authors who tend "to degrade one half of the human species, and render women pleasing at the expense of every solid virtue" (35). Constantly, he is invoked as the holder of opinions Wollstonecraft finds anathema; these include the idea that weakness in women is useful as a pretext for yielding to a natural appetite without violating romantic modesty, and the belief that girls from birth are naturally fond of adornment and gossip. Rousseau's woman is seen as a "fanciful kind of *half* being," one whose duties are directed only outward and who can work only through manipulating the passion of men.

By Chapter 5 Wollstonecraft is ready to deal at length with Rousseau as a writer who has "rendered women objects of pity, bordering on contempt." As she summarizes it, Rousseau's argument in *Emile* is that women ought to be weak and passive because they are physically weaker than men; they should be subordinate to men, to whom they must render themselves agreeable. To compensate for this dependence and inferiority, women have been given the facility to excite desire, through which men are made dependent. Female weakness enhances desirability and women are therefore quite right to glory in it. Rousseau asserts that the most important quality in a woman is good nature or sweetness of temper. Yet he appears to contradict this later when he considers that subtlety or animal cunning and sexual attractiveness are the only advantages of women to compare with men's physical strength and intellect. Wollstonecraft notes his contradiction, and laments the unhappy confusion it creates in the minds of women who are exhorted to cultivate good nature and yet are surrounded by examples of the success and power of cunning and seductiveness.

Having proved that men and women differ physically, mentally, and emotionally, Rousseau of course proposes different educational schemes for the sexes: "The education of the women should be always relative to the men," he asserts bluntly. "To please, to be useful to us, to make us love and esteem them, to educate us when young, and take care of us when grown up, to advise, to console us, to render our lives easy and agreeable: these arc the duties of women at all times, and what they should be taught in their infancy" (131). A harsh statement of male superiority, it is rendered outrageous by the insistance of the pronoun "us"; the author and his fellows pronounce definitively on women, the eternal other and object.

Continuing, Rousseau argues that physical development in boys is the development of physical power, whereas in girls it is the development of personal charm. In this way, adulthood extends its shadow over childhood. Because of their dependence girls must early learn restraint, since they will be subject to exercising it all their lives and must become used to doing so. This, in Rousseau's view, should not be difficult, because "a state of dependence being natural to the sex, they perceive themselves formed for obedience."

The commonplace nature of Rousseau's ideas emerges when Wollstonecraft discusses the works of Fordyce and Gregory, popular English educators who shared Rousseau's view of women's derivative nature. Again virtue and intelligence are useful only insofar as they attract men, and are a hindrance where they do not serve this end. The attacks on male writing about women that fill Chapter 5 reflect Wollstonecraft's view of the persuasive power of pedagogical and ethical works, especially when they reinforce an already widespread notion. Rousseau, termed in *The Wrongs of Woman* "the true Prometheus of feeling," is especially dangerous just because he is, like Burke, so powerful and emotional a writer. The pen on the side of prejudice is a lethal weapon.

The Argument of *The Rights of Woman*

Against the bias that gives birth to its own evidence, Wollstonecraft asserts the rights of women, especially to an education that would render them beings worthy of respect or at least immune to prejudice. Repeatedly, she stresses not equality of the sexes but the right of women to prove this through increased opportunities and independence. Although she provides rational bases for her arguments, they are in the main founded on religion; in Wollstonecraft's view, the degraded situation of women affronts the God who created men and women in his own image. To trivialize immortal souls through degrading reason becomes a most heinous crime against humanity.

Wollstonecraft fuses her rationalism and optimistic Christianity: reason becomes a proof of God and of human immortality. She argues from the belief that women possess reason and that this reason emanates from divinity and supports virtue. Although the quantity may vary, it is the same quality in all people: "The perfection of our nature and capability of happiness, must be estimated by the degree of reason, virtue, and knowledge, that distinguish the individual, and direct the laws which bind society: and that from the exercise of reason, knowledge and virtue naturally flow, is equally undeniable" (39).

In spite of the existence of reason in everyone, the women whom Wollstonecraft saw around her were certainly in her view inferior to men, both morally and intellectually. Moral inferiority has come from the idea of relative morality (so well expressed by Rousseau), which considers that women should order their conduct not to align it with absolute ethical standards but to please men. To this end, reason has been uncultivated in women, while sensibility or emotionalism has been allowed to grow excessively, to the point where it becomes lascivious indulgence. Virtue, to which people must aim, is seen as a balance through reason between restraint and emotion. So by concentrating only on the emotions, women have been cut off from rational virtue, a quality further obscured for them when female virtue is defined solely as sexual fidelity. Intellectual inferiority has come from faulty education that has termed unnatural any signs of robust thinking in women and has shut them out from any strenuous intellectual pursuits.[12]

The first page of Wollstonecraft's introduction well expresses the destructive process that renders women worthless creatures and then educates them accordingly:

The conduct and manners of women, in fact, evidently prove that their minds are not in a healthy state; for, like the flowers which are planted in too rich a soil, strength and usefulness are sacrificed to beauty; and the flaunting leaves, after having pleased a fastidious eye, fade, disregarded on the stalk, long before the season when they ought to have arrived at maturity.—One cause of this barren blooming I attribute to a false system of education, gathered from the books written on this subject by men who, considering females rather as women than human creatures, have been more anxious to make them alluring mistresses than affectionate wives and rational mothers; and the understanding of the sex has been so bubbled by this specious homage, that the civilized women of the present century, with a few exceptions, are only anxious to inspire love, when they ought to cherish a nobler ambition, and by their abilities and virtues exact respect. (31-32)

Clearly, the panacea for women's ills is education. It must, however, be education in reason, not the traditional triviality.

Pedagogy was one of the concerns of the century, and many debated whether a national education was desirable and feasible. Some saw it as the answer to a complexity of social and psychological ills, but William Godwin opposed it for boys and girls because he felt that education should be given only where it was actively sought and should never be imposed.[13] Wollstonecraft looked to the state for education of both sexes, since she felt it was the right of all. The universal education she envisioned was limited to the elementary level, after which some should proceed into vocational training according to their sex; the more able and affluent of both genders should continue with their education. She stressed the need for day schools that would complement a loving home. Her brief look at the boarding school of Eton had convinced her of the viciousness of the boarding system as practiced in England, where it reinforced both class and sex prejudices.

With education suitable for their class, women would, in Wollstonecraft's view, be able to support themselves adequately or fulfill themselves in their traditional role of wife and mother. Properly educated, they could prove themselves intellectually and morally equal to men; if they were neglected, such equality remained a hypothesis. The need for female education was a need also of society as a whole; unless the intellectual condition of women improved, there could be no further social advance for humanity.

To relate the subjection of women to the subjection of men under an arbitrary authority, Wollstonecraft cleverly brings together women and soldiers. Because both receive a deficient and harmful education, both often display the same characteristics. Because they are subordinated and because they enter the world prematurely, both have superficial knowledge, shallow characters, and a love of gallantry. What is said of soldiers can apply to women as well: "Society . . . as it becomes more enlightened, should be very careful not to establish bodies of men who must necessarily be made foolish or vicious by the very constitution of their profession." The profession of women, which their present education serves, is to be mistresses; but, like soldiers, women usually fill their function only for a very short period of their lives. In a stroke of genius that enforces her argument, Wollstonecraft compares the most "masculine" group of men with the most "feminine" group of women. Thus she makes her point about education and suggests the distortion behind the sexual labels: "Where is then the sexual difference," she demands, "when the education has been the same?"

Her Own Experience

Before she published *The Rights of Woman*, Wollstonecraft wrote to her friend William Roscoe that she was working on a book in which she herself would appear "head and heart."[14] Both are displayed when she treats the various classes of women, the pampered aristocrat, the bourgeois housewife or teacher, and the working woman or outcast.

Wollstonecraft reserves the harshest criticism in her book for the aristocratic woman who exists at the apex of two false systems of values, class and sex. Such a woman is marred by the effects of unjust privilege, both real from her upper-class position and illusory from her status as an object of sexual gallantry. She is both a parasite on society and its victim. As in *The Rights of Men*, here Wollstonecraft's hatred for this type of woman is certainly informed by her feelings toward Lady Kingsborough, the only aristocrat whose life she could have known intimately. Wollstonecraft came to the Kingsboroughs after her strenuous time at Newington Green as an independent, self-supporting and self-defining woman. The contrast between Lady Kingsborough and herself must have been keenly felt, the more so since it was not a simple contrast of passive dependence and active independence. In Wollstonecraft's letters, Lady Kingsborough was criticized not only for feminine passivity but also for her assumption of authority. In her Wollstonecraft encountered a harder problem than when she regarded the domestic woman of the middle class, and she responded harshly. In her writing, aristocratic women were mere animals, weak and depraved beings, fitting inmates of a seraglio. Clearly, she felt it useless to urge such women to take more care of their children or act as rational beings; the social situation that allowed their existence needed changing.

The horrors encountered by laboring women and servants, later forcibly illustrated in *The Wrongs of Woman*, are little discussed in *The Rights of Woman*. Wollstonecraft did, however, consider the plight of fallen women, a new group in her theoretical writings; she recommended that people treat them in an enlightened way and that their seducers maintain them:

I cannot avoid feeling the most lively compassion for those unfortunate females who are broken off from society, and by one error torn from all those affections and relationships that improve the heart and mind. It does not frequently even deserve the name of error; for many innocent girls become the dupes of a sincere, affectionate heart, and still more are, as it may emphatically be termed, *ruined* before they know the difference between virtue and vice:—and thus prepared by their education for infamy, they become infamous. Asylums and Magdalenes are not the proper remedies for these abuses. It is justice, not charity, that is wanting in the world! (165)

Wollstonecraft was not the first woman to plead for this group, but she was one of the first to make the problem part of a larger sexual and social condition and the fallen woman one of the victims—rather than the only victim—of social values. That she required justice rather than charity is a measure of her distance from *Original Stories*, where charity was often the only response to misery. Her knowledge of the working class cannot have been great, but her experience with the Bloods must have taught her how thin was the line between respectability and disgrace, between genteel and coarse poverty. Fanny Blood's sister crossed this line and ended in the workhouse, and the possibility of doing the same must have worried the Wollstonecraft sisters after the abduction of Eliza, when they anxiously discussed whether they could subsist on painting and sewing.

In depicting the middle class, Wollstonecraft had her own experience to draw on most fully. She had tried many of the routes open to women who could not or would not be dependent on their families. She had been a companion, a school teacher, and a governess. The liberality and kindness of Joseph Johnson had opened for her a profession rarely available to women, and her experience was so atypical that she did not suggest it as commonplace. In fact, she had little to say on the subject of the middle-class woman and employment, although she did in passing deplore the male intrusion into the traditionally female occupation of midwifery. She was more concerned with changing attitudes of women to allow them to see in their professional, intellectual, or domestic work the same possibility for fulfillment as men saw in theirs.

Like *Mary, A Fiction, The Rights of Woman* springs from Wollstonecraft's experience and does not escape its paradoxes: romantic love is seen as both a delusion and the "concomitant of genius"; an unhappy marriage is good for the children when contrasted with a passionate one, but disastrous when contrasted with one based on domestic friendship; sensibility marks the humanitarian and the languishing female. Such paradoxes reveal that right conduct is far from simple. Reason and its aid, education, are needed in large amounts for people of both sexes to make necessary fine judgments. If there is one absolute in the book that allows for no contradiction it is the need for reason in this situation. Chapter 1 opens with the ringing assertion that humanity's preeminence over animals is in reason, and the final chapter ends with an impassioned plea for the rights of reason for women.

In her own life in 1791 and 1792 Wollstonecraft needed the reason she praised, and her cry for it grew not only out of her past but out of her present. She was thirty-two, still in a way isolated, unloved, and, although famous, unappreciated. Over the months Fuseli had come to stand for the intellectual stimulation and the emotional warmth she required, and her infatuation had grown apace. While writing her book she was exhilarated by her own courage in love and literature; when she finished, however, she sank into the restlessness and dissatisfaction that so often plagued the dependent women she described. "Her pen was palsied," Johnson later told Godwin. "You know the cause."

Certainly the intensity of her passion for Fuseli must have come from her years of repressed emotion, her often exaggerated care of an importunate family. It sprang too from female dependence on the social forms that she castigated in *The Rights of Woman*. A passionate act that affronted these forms was so horrifying that everyone recoiled from it and branded the woman an outcast. When Wollstonecraft knocked on the door, announced to his wife she could no longer live without Fuseli, and begged to be admitted into the family, she committed such an act. After her rejection she had little to do but leave for a liberated France. There she tested the theories of *The Rights of Woman* in her own life and for a time sadly depicted in herself the picture of the subservient female, trained deeply in sensibility, not self-respect.

Reaction to the Book

The Rights of Woman was widely read, but it is difficult to gauge its effect. Some opponents countered with abuse and burlesque in such works as *A Vindication of the Rights of Brutes* and *A Sketch of the Rights of Boys and Girls*. Horace Walpole classed Wollstonecraft with Paine as one of "the philosophizing serpents we have in our bosom," and Wollstonecraft's sister quoted a popular view of the book as "the most indecent Rhapsody that ever was penned by man or woman."[15] The opposite reaction can be seen in Robert Southey's dedication to his poem "The Triumph of Woman" and in Mary Hays's preface in her *Letters and Essays*, in which she praises the virtues, talents, and daring of Wollstonecraft's book.[16]

Some years later Mary Hays was even more enthusiastic and in her obituary notice she extolled *The Rights of Woman,* where Wollstonecraft had, in her words, labored "to awaken in the minds of her oppressed sex a sense of their degradation, and to restore them to the dignity of reason and virtue."[17] Later, as the times became more conservative, Hays grew less fervent, finding fault with the style, arrangement, and even occasional coarseness of the book. Yet ultimately she continued to admire the courage and power of a writer who had dared to show her oppressors "the various means and arts by which woman had been forcibly subjugated, flattered into imbecility, and invariably held in bondage." She concluded justly of Wollstonecraft and her controversial work: "To advance on the scale of reason half the species, is no ignoble ambition."[18]

The reaction of contemporary journals was predictable: the radical publications were enthusiastic, the more conventional were hostile. The *Critical Review* concluded that there must be something rotten in Wollstonecraft's reasoning since her results were so offensive, and it advised the author to seek delicacy, elegance, and sensibility so that she might grow pleasing and achieve happiness. It forcibly objected to the book's crude style, describing it as flowery, flowing, weak, and confused.[19]

A more balanced opinion came from the *Monthly Review*, which approved much of the work, commending Wollstonecraft's efforts to raise women from their degraded state and supporting her desire for female modesty and reason. The journal did, however, doubt the wisdom of some of her ideas, especially of women's entering into civil government, a project it considered rather romantic.[20]

Praise came of course from Wollstonecraft's own *Analytical Review*, which lauded the author for recognizing how men have turned women into sexual objects and for daring to put forward her radical views at all. If the ideas of *The Rights of Woman* were implemented, the reviewer asserted, the country would be a better and happier place.[21]

A few years later, when Wollstonecraft's scandalous life became public through Godwin's *Memoirs*, the reviews of *The Rights of Woman* grew overwhelmingly hostile. The *Anti-Jacobin Review* in 1798 not only castigated the book's ideas but dismissed them as superficial and derivative.[22] The *Lady's Monthly Museum* went further by exemplifying the horrible effect of the book in a letter said to be from an indignant mother. This woman bewailed Wollstonecraft's power over her unsexed daughters, one of whom had gone hunting; another had taken up ancient philosophy, another anatomy, while the last one had begun swearing like a man.[23]

Even more dreadful fates awaited women in the spate of cautionary novels of the late eighteenth century. In George Walker's *The Vagabond*, for example, the chief character Mary is tarnished with Wollstonecraft's sentiments; she is described as a prostitute available to any man who wants her. In case the connection with *The Rights of Woman* remained unclear, Walker directed the reader to the book in footnotes.[24] Similarly, in the anonymous *Robert and Adela* Lady Susan is corrupted by Wollstonecraft's work, although she is finally reformed and cured of the evil. In this novel one character is given the opinion that "Mrs. Woolstone Croft" would never have written such a book had she been a fulfilled woman, a happy wife and mother.[25]

Chapter Six

The French Revolution

Long before she went to France, Wollstonecraft was intrigued by French events and, in the years following the fall of the Bastille, showed she had definite ideas about the revolutionary upsurge across the Channel. When she arrived in Paris in 1792 she was ready to judge the political situation according to already formed opinions. Certainly she was aware of the need to judge correctly, for the Revolution was the test of the radical political views she held so dear. She came to France with set opinions; she also came with the emotional scars of her abortive liaison with Fuseli.

An Historical and Moral View of the Origin and Progress of the French Revolution, and the Effect it Has Produced in Europe was the first volume of a projected series on the history of France, which was never completed.[1] It concerns only the events of the early months of the Revolution in 1789; the actions of the National Assembly, the efforts of Necker to contain the growing popular fury, the speeches and decisions of such leaders as Mirabeau and Lafayette, the storming of the Bastille on July 14, and the people's march to Versailles on October 5. The book was finished in April 1794, however, and thus grew out of Wollstonecraft's knowledge of the later violent events of the Jacobin period under Robespierre.

She takes the facts of her history primarily from French government records and from English periodicals, but her comments, which fill a large portion of the book, are her own, reflecting the changing times and the upheavals of her personal life. The view that emerges is an evolutionary one; the Revolution becomes the natural consequence of intellectual progress and, despite its violence and barbarity, the sign of genuine improvement for France and ultimately for all of Europe. It is a hopeful conclusion, certainly at odds with the tenor of much of the book.

Early Reactions

Wollstonecraft's progress toward understanding the Revolution was slow. In *The Rights of Men* she had shown a rather abstract interest in French theory and practice, but in the months before her arrival in France she was increasingly concerned with actual events. She frequently reviewed French works and her choice of quotations from them suggests passages in her later book. In a review of Madame Sillery Brulat's *Leçons d'une Gouvernante*, for example, she notes that the book reveals the servility of the French character owing to despotism; this became a frequent theme in her later work, for it helped to explain the excesses of the Revolution. Again, in a review of the *Letters of the Countess du Barré* she mentions the "*glorious* labours" of the National Assembly, which is called "that *patriotic body*"; in *The French Revolution* Wollstonecraft warmly expresses her admiration for the Assembly.[2]

The ultimately optimistic view of the Revolution that she reveals in her history and to some extent in her reviews was not always evident. Arriving in France late in 1792, dejected and needing both personal and ideological comfort, she was immediately disappointed and disapproving. Indeed, she was so shaken by the reality of a situation she had never fully understood that she responded almost as Burke had responded when in *Reflections* he had visualized the humiliation of the French queen. It was a response she had vigorously denounced; ironically, it is conveyed in one of her finest pieces of prose.

From her window Wollstonecraft saw Louis XVI passing to his trial and she was moved by the sight. Almost at once she sat down to describe to Joseph Johnson what she had seen and felt, and she skillfully blends the event, personal response, and rhetorical patterning:

About nine o'clock this morning, the king passed by my window, moving silently along (excepting now and then a few strokes on the drum, which rendered the stillness more awful) through empty streets, surrounded by the national guards, who, clustering round the carriage, seemed to deserve their name. The inhabitants flocked to their windows, but the casements were all shut, not a voice was heard, nor did I see any thing like an insulting gesture.—For the first time since I entered France, I bowed to the majesty of the people, and respected the propriety of behaviour so perfectly in unison with my own feelings. I can scarcely tell you why, but an association of ideas made the tears flow insensibly from my eyes, when I saw Louis sitting, with more dignity than I expected from his character, in a hackney coach, going to meet death, where so many of his race have triumphed. . . . I wish I had even kept the cat with me!—I want to see something alive; death in so many frightful shapes has taken hold of my fancy.—I am going to bed—and, for the first time in my life, I cannot put out the candle.[3]

In this passage, she sympathizes with the king as a person and pities the human tragedy that was part of the Revolution. Such reactions are absent from her book. Perhaps she was afraid of their effect, since in her earlier treatment of Burke she had shown herself quite aware of the tremendous power of sympathy and compassion to overwhelm reason. It is probable that through her work she wished to prevent others from giving way to the pessimism to which such emotions would inevitably lead. She must indeed have been alive to the danger, for she herself became disheartened a few weeks after she wrote the account. Her pessimism is expressed in the "Letter on the Present Character of the French Nation," sent to Joseph Johnson but not published until after her death.[4]

In the "Letter" Wollstonecraft sadly renounced her rationalist faith in human progress and the revolutionary belief in the efficacy of sudden political and social change she had inherited from Price. She wrote of the despair with which she contemplated vices, follies, and prejudice instead of the "fair form of Liberty . . . and Virtue." She feared that the aristocracy of birth she had so harshly criticized in *The Rights of Men* had been replaced not by equality but by an aristocracy of riches even more destructive to freedom and dignity than the old order. She showed her loss of faith in the possibility of people's working simply for virtue without the spur of misery. In the depth of her disappointment she cried that the theory of perfectibility had failed and that vice and evil were in reality the "grand mobile of action." Civilization and virtue, once firmly joined, now seemed incompatible, and the revolutionary effort at joining them was found to have destroyed both. The radical difference between these opinions and those expressed in *The Rights of Men* is clear. Wollstonecraft had some reason to exhort the readers of her later history to guard against judgment based on emotions. She had proved the results with her own experience.

By the time she wrote *The French Revolution* her emotional despair had been partly conquered; she had in the main regained her rationalist faith in humanity, although frequently her descriptions of events jar with her optimistic rationalist interpretations of them. Her partial success was certainly not due to the happier course of events, for the period after she arrived in France and before she completed her manuscript was one of the bloodiest of the Revolution. The purges of Robespierre had begun and she lived through the deaths of many of her girondist friends. She had seen the pavements of Paris wet with the blood of the victims and had been silenced when moved to exclaim against the sight. What the change in opinion indicated was an intellectual struggle, of which the outcome was a reaffirmation of a faith long held. *The French Revolution* represented a more or less successful assimilation of painful facts into a preformed faith. The achievement was the more remarkable when one remembers that, as she wrote her history, she was beginning on the long agony of her disintegrating affair with Imlay, a time singularly inappropriate for an ideological struggle.

Background

Wollstonecraft's history was one of many that attempted to interpret the Revolution to an eager English audience. Indeed, more writing on the subject was produced in England before 1800 than in any decade of the nineteenth century.[5] All the accounts were similar in their attempts to judge and understand before the course of the Revolution had become clear. Among the early works, only the *Annual Register* urged the necessity of gathering and organizing the facts before building elaborate theories upon them. The first ten years of comment in England produced primarily propaganda and imaginative literature as well as the great polemical works, which although they concerned the Revolution, were primarily studies in political theory, such as Godwin's *Political Justice* and the two works that grew out of the Price controversy, Burke's *Reflections on the Revolution in France* and Paine's *Rights of Man.*

Wollstonecraft's view of the events resembles that of a few other writers. The most important of these are Arthur Young and her friend Helen Maria Williams, the first of whose many books on France Wollstonecraft reviewed for the *Analytical Review* in 1790. Both authors described events as they occurred and so revealed in their works the struggle that Wollstonecraft suggested, if all her treatments of the Revolution are taken together. Like Wollstonecraft, Young at first saw the necessity of change in a France sunk under despotism, but by 1793 he had become convinced that the changes had been too radical. He blamed the bloodshed partly on the earlier despotism—as Wollstonecraft does in her work—and partly on the nature of mobs. Unlike Wollstonecraft, Young turned against the application of any theory in government.[6]

Helen Maria Williams wrote one of the most detailed accounts of those turbulent years. She resembled Wollstonecraft in being initially confused by the revolutionary cruelty, which she did not anticipate. Since she suffered from it directly, as Wollstonecraft did not, her confusion was all the more overwhelming. Nonetheless, she managed to reach a position from which she could condemn the Terror while retaining a more cautious belief in a final improvement in human liberty.[7]

Possibly Wollstonecraft knew the work of Young and the later work of Williams, although she did not refer to either in her book. Instead, she mainly used the *New Annual Register*, a record written each year in England for posterity (often by William Godwin) in imitation of the better-known but ideologically distinct *Annual Register*. Its preface of 1780 stated that the editors had endeavored to present the material with "perspicuity, copiousness, and impartiality." Its stand on the early revolutionary years, however, was clearly pre-revolutionary and antimonarchical, for in the volume of 1790 the people of France were described glowingly as "enlightened" and "impregnated" with the desire for liberty." By 1794, however, the *New Annual Register* was objecting to the jacobin purges, while at the same time condemning British efforts to "punish" France through war. Its position on the events of 1789 was very close to Wollstonecraft's.[8]

The writing of *The French Revolution* took place against a backdrop of historical and emotional upheavals. Wollstonecraft began it in 1793 at Neuilly, the little village to which she had fled after the fall of the girondins and the general round-up of the British. She had escaped imprisonment when Imlay falsely registered her as his wife, but her fellow historian Helen Maria Williams had been taken. When Williams was released she warned her friend of the dangers of publishing indiscreet opinions or indeed of writing any opinions at all. But Wollstonecraft was undeterred. Perhaps she was pushed by financial pressure; she had constant drains on her money and was often in difficulties in France, although primarily because her income from Johnson did not always arrive. More likely, however, she wrote to escape from the melancholy fear of Imlay's cooling that plagued and soured her letters. "Do not turn from me," she constantly implored him, although she must have suspected that he had.

While composing the book Wollstonecraft was trailing after Imlay, first to Paris from Neuilly, and then, without special invitation, from Paris to Le Havre where he had gone on business. To make matters worse, she was pregnant, and however the French might have regarded illegitimacy, the British definitely looked at it askance. By the time Imlay left Le Havre for Paris again in 1794, she seems temporarily to have renewed confidence in him, and her letters, although still occasionally imploring, are predominantly loving and tender. While Imlay was away, she completed her history of the Revolution, the only book from which she rigorously excluded overt reference to her own emotional experiences. In the circumstances the exclusion must have cost her a great deal.

The Argument of *The French Revolution*

The preface and title of Wollstonecraft's book, *An Historical and Moral View of the . . . French Revolution*, indicate that the work is not a straightforward account of events. In her preface she mentions the bloody events of the present and admits the chilling effect that reports of these have had on her sympathy with the early Revolution. Her book is to be an aid in aligning the views with reason and guarding against the "erroneous inferences of sensibility."

The French Revolution confirms the stand taken by Wollstonecraft in *The Rights of Men.* It aims to prove that the revolutionary brutalities were due not to any inherent weakness in rationalist philosophy but to the degraded character of the French people, too long subject to a despotic and feudal government. Her sketch of history before the Revolution is designed to make this point. The chief fault she finds in the French is excessive sensibility—the emotionalism she had earlier attacked in Burke and that she had so clearly displayed herself in *Mary, A Fiction.*

Throughout her book, Wollstonecraft explores her strong rationalist belief in reason and morality: "It is morals, not feeling, which distinguish men from the beasts of prey." The French had too much affected feeling and insufficient morality to conclude a successful revolution; the debilitating effects of the past were too strong to be removed quickly, and the Terror occurred when they insisted on a freedom far beyond their capacity. The French, like Burke, are characterized as loving theatrical show, the result of their indulged feelings: "Their national character is, perhaps, more formed by their theatrical amusements, than is generally imagined," Wollstonecraft primly asserts; "they are in reality the schools of vanity. And, after this kind of education, is it surprising, that almost every thing is said and done for stage effect? or that cold declamatory extasies blaze forth, only to mock the expectation with a show of warmth?"[9] In her view, such shallowness of emotion can easily manifest itself in cruelty.

Since French depravity, not human depravity, had caused the temporary failure of the Revolution, the rest of humanity need not be considered damned. A people governed by reason could successfully conclude what the impulsive and self-indulgent French had marred. Wollstonecraft is as emphatically opposed to the idea of universal inadequacy and depravity—dismissed as the "wild traditions of original sin"—as when she first crossed swords with Burke.

While admitting that the French Revolution has temporarily failed, Wollstonecraft stresses that it was successful if viewed from the perspective of French history. In this context, the chaos of the present is justified as inevitable and ultimately beneficial; it will finally result in a freer environment for the common people, which in turn must result in improvement in their character:

From implicitly obeying their sovereigns, the french became suddenly all sovereigns; yet, because it is natural for men to run out of one extreme into another, we should guard against inferring, that the spirit of the moment will not evaporate, and leave the disturbed water more clear for the fermentation. Men without principle rise like foam during a storm sparkling on the top of the billow, in which it is soon absorbed when the commotion dies away. Anarchy is a fearful state, and all men of sense and benevolence have been anxiously attentive, to observe what use frenchmen would make of their liberty, when the confusion incident to the acquisition should subside: yet, whilst the heart sickens over a detail of crimes and follies ... it is perhaps, difficult to bring ourselves to believe, that out of this chaotic mass a fairer government is rising than has ever shed the sweets of social life on the world. (72-73)

Wollstonecraft could hold this view because she had committed herself as firmly as ever to the belief that a free environment would finally make a free people, and that humanity, although it might suffer setbacks, was still ultimately perfectable. Certainly, however, it is special pleading. It may not be too fanciful to find in this imposition of rationalism onto the chaos of indulged emotion a parallel to her efforts at rationally controlling her frantic infatuation with the retreating Imlay.

The political and social ideas first set forth in *The Rights of Men* are repeated in *The French Revolution*, and many of the passages seem interchangeable. As in the earlier book, Wollstonecraft inveighs forcefully against hereditary rank and wealth: "Civilization hitherto, by producing the inequality of conditions, which makes wealth more desirable than either talents or virtue, has so weakened all the organs of the body-politic, and rendered man such a beast of prey, that the strong have always devoured the weak till the very signification of justice has been lost sight of, and charity, the most specious system of slavery, substituted in it's place. . . . People are rendered ferocious by misery; and misanthropy is ever the offspring of discontent." She ends with a plea that might refer to the oppressed, to women, and indeed to herself in her emotional servitude: "Let not then the happiness of one half of mankind be built on the misery of the other" (71).

Again she proclaims her belief in social progress: "It is a vulgar error, built on a superficial view of the subject," she declares firmly, ". . . that civilization can only go as far as it has hitherto gone, and then must necessarily fall into barbarism. Yet this much appears certain, that a state will infallibly grow old and feeble, if hereditary riches support hereditary rank, under any description. But when courts and primogeniture are done away, and simple equal laws are established, what is to prevent each generation from retaining the vigour of youth?" (19-20). There is not here, as there is in *The Rights of Men*, the insistent presence of brother Edward, but it is hard to ignore Wollstonecraft's wasted and untutored youth when reading these words. The stranglehold of the courts on the oppressed would engross her more fully in her last work, *The Wrongs of Woman*.

As in *The Rights of Men*, reason, the foundation of human perfectibility, is still a faculty shared with God. *The French Revolution* differs, however, from the earlier book in significantly diminished emphasis on the divine plan for creation. Indeed, it seems that the God Wollstonecraft posits here is little more than the inward pattern of reason, "the image of God implanted in our nature": "One principal of action is sufficient—Respect thyself—whether it be termed fear of God—religion; love of justice—morality; or, self-love—the desire of happiness" (18). It appears that belief in reason has survived the horrors of the Revolution and the miseries of Wollstonecraft's own experience, but that trust in an all-knowing and all-loving God, so present as comfort in the early works, has been a victim of the onslaught.

In one respect her ideas seem clearly accelerated by her personal experience. Imlay was a trader—in "alum or soap" as she contemptuously writes in one letter—and he either desired to get rich through this trade or used it to avoid revealing his increasing detachment from Wollstonecraft. Naturally, she seized on this rival—one slightly less painful than the women he was openly involved with later—and lashed out both in her letters and in *The French Revolution* against trade. Commerce, she concluded, degraded masters and works alike; it rendered the former selfish and turned the latter into servile "manufacturers rather than husbandmen," people whose minds decayed through mental inactivity and constant subservience. She argued brilliantly against that division of labor on which industrialism and commerce rested: "The time which . . . is sauntered away, in going from one part of an employment to another, is the very time that preserves the man from degenerating into a brute . . . whole knots of men [are] turned into machines, to enable a keen speculator to become wealthy; and every noble principle of nature is eradicated by making a man pass his life in stretching wire, pointing a pin, heading a nail, or spreading a sheet of paper on a plain surface" (519) Life in Le Havre with the speculating Imlay and his trading friends must frequently have been uncomfortable for both partners.

As much as *The French Revolution* continues the philosophical trends of the two *Vindications*, in one notable respect it differs markedly from them. On the basis of the earlier works, one would expect Wollstonecraft to stress the part played by women in the Revolution, but surprisingly she hardly mentions female heroism; in fact she uses the word "women" pejoratively in a way she had largely avoided in *The Rights of Woman*.[10]

After inveighing against aristocratic women in both *Vindications*,

Wollstonecraft predictably attacks the arch-aristocrat, Marie Antoinette, who inspires her with the sort of bitterness and disgust earlier reserved for Lady Kingsborough. What is unexpected, however, is the harshness she shows when she treats the laboring-class women who marched to Versailles, a throwback to her harshness toward servants in *Thoughts*. The march, which ended in the removal of the king to Paris, had been castigated by Burke and defended by Wollstonecraft as a necessary if unfortunate event in the Revolution; here, however, she sounds closer to Burke than to her former self: "The concourse, at first, consisted mostly of market women, and the lowest refuse of the streets, women who had thrown off the virtues of one sex without having power to assume more than the vices of the other. . . . they were strictly speaking a mob, affixing all the odium to the appellation it can possibly import; and not to be confounded with the honest multitude, who took the Bastille" (426). The description of the action is equally hostile: "Uttering a loud and general cry, they hurled a volley of stones at the soldiers, who, unwilling, or ashamed, to fire on women, though with the appearance of furies, retreated into the hall." The inspiration of the women in Wollstonecraft's account is neither the shortage of food nor the soaring prices, but the gold of the Duke of Orleans, who wished to use the female mob for his own nefarious ends. Burke went no further in his indictment.

The treatment of women in *The French Revolution* is not entirely harsh. Indeed, there are comments throughout that echo passages in *The Rights of Woman* concerning the unique injustices suffered by the female sex. Yet, since Wollstonecraft characteristically makes her point through emphasis, repetition, and mounting rhetoric, such isolated instances do not remain in the reader's mind and do not outweigh the set pieces on Marie Antoinette and the marchers to Versailles.[11]

Perhaps it is best to assume that in *The French Revolution* Wollstonecraft's feminist theory followed her political one. She had to struggle to assimilate a complicated and often repulsive political reality in a preconceived system of thought; in similar manner, she had to battle with the unexpected situation of women acting in unfamiliar and threatening ways before she could transcend it to see all women in the light of her earlier feminist theory. In her personal life her growing fears of Imlay's infidelity also no doubt contributed to a lack of sympathy with women. Her enormous insecurity about his love could well have alienated her from her own sex, leading her to see all women as possible rivals.

Another factor in the treatment of the march to Versailles may also have been Wollstonecraft's class sympathies. In her description she pitted the laboring servants and market women against the "honest" petty bourgeois stormers of the Bastille, with whom she had far more kindred feelings. Only in the later *Letters from Sweden* did her contempt for "the lowest refuse" of society diminish, and only in *The Wrongs of Woman*, her last work, did she transcend both general and personal fears to portray with sympathy the peculiar horror suffered by women of the laboring class.

Style

In its defects and felicities, the style of *The French Revolution* is similar to that of Wollstonecraft's other works. The book is full of florid biological images so much a part of the two *Vindications*. Anarchy, for example, becomes "the excrementitious humours exuding from the contaminated body," while tyranny draws "the vital juice of labour, to fill the insatiable jaws of thousands of fawning slaves and sycophants." Such baroque images now seem distasteful, but they support one of her main perceptions, that countries and individuals grow and age alike. The psychology of a person is for her the psychology of a nation: both move from infancy through adolescent turbulence to the political freedom of maturity. As a person's defects of character result from faulty domestic education, so a nation's errors stem from faulty government.[12]

As in the two *Vindications*, Wollstonecraft's polemical aim gave rise to frequent rhetorical passages full of alliteration, parallelism, and extended metaphor. The most outstanding of these is the long description of Versailles, the palace of the dead king:

How silent is now Versailles!—The solitary foot, that mounts the sumptuous stair-case, rests on each landing-place, whilst the eye traverses the void, almost expecting to see the strong images of fancy burst into life.— The train of the Louises, like the posterity of the Banquoes, pass in solemn sadness, pointing at the nothingness of grandeur, fading away on the cold canvas, which covers the nakedness of the spacious walls—whilst the gloominess of the atmosphere gives a deeper shade to the gigantic figures, that seem to be sinking into the embraces of death.

Warily entering the endless apartments, half shut up, the fleeting shadow of the pensive wanderer, reflected in long glasses, that vainly gleam in every direction, slacken the nerves, without appalling the heart. . . . The very air is chill, seeming to clog the breath; and the wasting dampness of destruction appears to be stealing into the vast pile, on every side. (161-162)

The passage continues with a dirge for France, with the author an element in a tableau, the weeper for a nation that is gone. The passage is dignified and moderately effective, but the rhetorical posturing seems hollow in comparison with the controlled personal emotion so successfully expressed in the letter to Johnson on the king's passing. It remains to the end a set piece, and the emotions it conveys seem forced and conventional.

But much of the work is free from such posturing and overwriting. It is written clearly and there is a continuity of paragraph and section that is often lacking in Wollstonecraft's other books, which suggests that she could respond well to a limitation of subject matter. Many similes are apt and thought provoking, for example, the comparison of court pageantry to a harlot's ornaments: "Constrained by the *etiquette*, which made the principal part of the imposing grandeur of Louis XIV, the queen wished to throw aside the cumbersome brocade of ceremony, without having discernment enough to perceive, that it was necessary to lend mock dignity to a court, where there was not sufficient virtue, or native beauty to give interest or respectability to simplicity. The harlot is seldom such a fool as to neglect her meretricious ornaments, unless she renounces her trade; and the pageantry of courts is the same thing on a larger scale" (34-35).

The shorter remarks also illuminate. Of the queen, Wollstonecraft writes perceptively: "If she felt some touches of sympathy, it was only the unison of the moment." With such comments, the book comes alive and a dry recitation of events turns into an experience of them.

Reaction to the Book

In spite of the apparent perversity of its thesis, *The French Revolution* was quite well received in England.[13] A second edition was published in 1795. Reaction in periodicals was fairly predictable, for

Wollstonecraft was by this time a writer of some note and notoriety (although the full enormity of her personal life was not yet flaunted before the public) and the ideological battle lines in Britain were clear. The conservative journals were on the whole hostile, criticizing both her interpretations and her heavy dependence for facts on the *New Annual Register*, certainly a serious weakness of the history. The less conservative publications commended the interpretations, facts, and even the style.[14]

In the subsequent two centuries *The French Revolution* had no great following. Its mixture of polemic and topicality has dated it more than the other works, and its relative lack of personal allusions, whatever the cause, has made it unappealing to students of Wollstonecraft's life. Yet the work, her longest, is valuable within her own canon as the best expression of her peculiar combination of opinion, analysis, and literary expression, and in a wider literary context as a contemporary reaction to French events. In addition, it has had several famous students, some of whom appear to have been influenced by its viewpoint. Among these were John Adams, who read the work attentively and then pronounced its author "a Lady of a masculine masterly Understanding."[15] He admired the enthusiasm with which she set forth her vision of perfectibility, and his admiration was not lessened by his difference of opinion. Adams retained a belief in an aristocracy of merit where Wollstonecraft's experience of the French Revolution had convinced her of its danger; she kept her belief in the absolute power of virtue, about which Adams had grown extremely skeptical.

Another student of the book was Wollstonecraft's son-in-law, the poet Percy Bysshe Shelley. He seems primarily to have been struck by the explanation of the temporary failure of the Revolution; probably it influenced him to see his main political task not as bringing about a revolution in England but as preparing people's minds for it.[16]

On Wollstonecraft herself, the completion of *The French Revolution* seems to have had less effect than the conclusion of the two *Vindications*. After *The Rights of Men* she had triumphed in her literary powers; after *The Rights of Woman* she had grown depressed by personal and literary failings. *The French Revolution* came out amid such confusion of politics and emotions that its publication seems scarcely to have touched her. Yet its writing covertly revealed much about her life and obsessions. Occasionally, as in the treatment of women and trade, it seems a fairly straightforward reflection of her own tormented feelings. In other cases the reflection is inverted, as when she turns the deep pessimism of her personal life into the strained optimism of the history, or when she denigrates the trivial and immoral French in the book while in her letters praising them in comparison to the serious British.

Undoubtedly, the project of writing this book helped to keep Wollstonecraft sane in a time of domestic and social turmoil. Sadly, however, the ideological struggle to hold to certain views against hope and even sometimes against experience was fitting her for the demoralizing battle against the knowledge that Imlay had rejected her. The ultimate optimism of *The French Revolution*, so qualified even in its closing chapters, is more darkly undercut when the book is placed in the context of Wollstonecraft's life. Perhaps it is fortunate in being the only one of her later works that does not insist on this context.

Chapter Seven

Letters from Sweden

"If ever there was a book calculated to make a man in love with its author, this appears to me to be the book."[1] This comment sums up William Godwin's opinion of *Letters Written During a Short Residence in Sweden, Norway, and Denmark*, Mary Wollstonecraft's least polemical and most appealing work. Nowadays readers will concur with Godwin's glowing assessment, and Ralph Wardle judges this to be Wollstonecraft's "most mature and most delightful book."[2] Carol Poston finds it "quite possibly the perfect fusion of the personal and intellectual selves of Mary Wollstonecraft,"[3] and even Claire Tomalin, one of the least sympathetic modern biographers of Wollstonecraft, pronounces her "a good travel writer."[4]

Many factors account for the popularity and enduring strength of *Letters from Sweden*, especially its range and rich content. Wollstonecraft delights in nature, is relaxed yet alert in unfamiliar terrain, and showers us, often anecdotally, with special asides and political judgment.

A major trauma in her life generated the work's energy, for Wollstonecraft had been sent to Scandinavia as Gilbert Imlay's business agent to help her recover from her first serious attempt at suicide. *Letters from Sweden* unveiled a bewildered state of mind in which she loathed to see as well as longed to return to her indifferent lover. Once she escaped her troubles at least geographically, however, she seems to have transcended her unsettled private life; her tour of Scandinavia, after all, demanded no dealings with her disquieting past unless she chose to write to Imlay. Moreover, the act of writing afforded her the intimate contact she so desperately craved, but could not physically achieve. Ironically, the fact that the trip itself necessarily kept her apart from Imlay sedated her nerves. The worry of rejection disappeared for the moment.

Not part of an eighteenth-century grand tour of Europe, Scandinavia provided Wollstonecraft with an abundance of experiences,

generally unknown even to well-traveled Britishers. This partly inspired her to write about her tour, for when she could, she was always
one to turn her experiences into written form. In the past, she had
written works on education because her belief in its necessity absorbed
her; then as the development of ideas became her preoccupation, she
joined the ranks of polemicists. On this occasion, she decided to chronicle the adventures prompted by psychological and physical needs to
restore body and mind. Consequently, Wollstonecraft was integrating
many levels of her life in *Letters from Sweden*. Using the form of a
personal journal-monologue addressed to Imlay, a style of writing
rarely to be found in her works as a whole, she churned out facts
and tales about the countries and people of Scandinavia liberally inter-
laced with political commentary, philosophical observations, and reports on her continuing sorrow over wasted affections.

Together with *Letters from Sweden*, which Joseph Johnson com-
missioned for publication in 1796, she engaged in a more private
correspondence with Imlay that consisted of more than a hundred
letters.[5] Seventy-seven of these were later published by William Godwin as *Letters* in his collection of Wollstonecraft's posthumous works
(they are subsequently referred to by their more common title, *Letters
to Imlay*). These obviously overlapped with *Letters from Sweden*,
yet one striking difference between the two sets lies in Wollstonecraft's degree of involvement with Imlay. *Letters to Imlay* reveals her
immediate direct response to an emotionally devastating relationship,
while *Letters from Sweden* exposes a preoccupying anxiety and a
continuing love but in the wider context of her Scandinavian experiences: she addresses Imlay directly only a few times but we sense her
presence through the easy familiarity of her style; often she speaks as
if she were confiding her feelings and responses to a favored friend.
On the other hand at the end of Letter IX, she questions "whether
I ought to rejoice at having turned over in this solitude a new page
in the history of my own heart, though I may venture to assure you
that a further acquaintance with mankind only tends to increase my
respect for your judgment and esteem for your character" (91). To
Imlay and the public, Wollstonecraft proclaims her conflict and the
difficulty she has in controlling her feelings. Only her private letters
reveal how feelings threaten to engulf her. She is in a sense using this
epistolary journal of her travels, her art, to cope, to come to terms,
even (if only subconsciously) to distance herself. Her closing lines

underscore that difficulty: "Thoughts . . . lie too close to my heart
to be easily shook off."

In *Letters from Sweden* she focuses on her journey, treating her
relationship with Imlay as a theme in a minor key. In *Letters to Imlay*
she records the deterioration of their relationship set against the backdrop of continental sojourns in Scandinavia and beyond. The difference between her seeming control in one volume and her absence of
control to the point of suicide in the other bespeaks a divided Wollstonecraft, although through it all she remains a woman who has
begun to transform the raw elements of grief into art.

Despite her greater assurance and self-control in *Letters from
Sweden*, however, she (perhaps unconsciously) magnetizes the reader's sympathy. To read the private *Letters to Imlay* is to intrude, but to
read *Letters from Sweden* is to be invited to share and to empathize.
She frequently exposes her most intimate feelings and airs the results
of her all-encompassing self-scrutiny: "What a long time it requires
to know ourselves. I cannot immediately determine whether I ought
to rejoice at having turned over in this solitude a page in the history
of my own heart" (90-91). The revelatory quality of *Letters from
Sweden* ensures Wollstonecraft a prominent place in any history of
the confessional, one of the typical forms of women's literature.[6] The
book spans the time between letters XL of *Letters to Imlay*, in which
she apologizes for having inconvenienced him by her first suicide
attempt, and LXVII, which she writes on the verge of another. These
twenty-five letters reveal a deeply wounded Wollstonecraft who is
minimizing her anguish (consciously or not) by writing about her
experiences in a public mode, too proud to bare the pain except in
muted conclusions and occasional interjections. She cannot yet "estimate everything at its just value" as Godwin later counselled her.

Her announcement of the aim and plan of her letter in the prefatory "Advertisement" makes her self-consciousness plain. She uncovers
her process: when she corrected for the over-intrusion of self, her
writing became too studied. Eventually she found her 'golden mean':
"I, therefore, determined to let my remarks and reflections flow unrestrained, as I perceived that I could not give a just description of
what I saw, but by relating the effect different objects had produced
on my mind and feelings, whilst the impression was still fresh."
Clearly she means to write a thoroughly subjectivist appreciation, "a
just view of the present state of the countries I have passed through

. . . avoiding those details which . . . appear very insipid" (6); she
does not intend to expose personal turmoil, however. In that sense the
book is a model of tender restraint.

Wollstonecraft continually deviates from her avowed plan to write
a travelogue that can double as an essay promoting intellectual inquiry. As she addresses Imlay, she backtracks, frequently digresses, lux-
uriates in her feelings, and seeks rapprochement through emotional
bonding. In this sense, *Letters from Sweden* is as much the record of
a personal relationship as is *Mary, A Fiction*. Wollstonecraft bluntly
acknowledges that constant emotional difficulties have obstructed her
original purpose. In the appendix she explains apologetically, "Private
business and cares have frequently so absorbed me, as to prevent my
obtaining all the information, during this journey, which the novelty
of the scenes would have afforded, had my attention been continually
awake to inquiry" (197).

Letters from Sweden as a Bridge to Imlay

Wollstonecraft made strenuous yet subtle efforts to reknit her relationship with Imlay. She sought in *Letters from Sweden* to reach
him through references to the geography and topography of Scandinavia, two subjects that so fascinated him that he had earlier written
a book on North American topography.[7] She also attempted to revital-
ize her love through sheer intellectual energy, vivacity, and often and
probably least successfully, through tortured litanies itemizing her
melancholy.

She reproves Imlay for her sufferings, discomfits him with stories
of her fatigue and disorders, while petulantly (and paradoxically)
reminding him that she does not complain. In an apparent attempt
to reforge their emotional links, she attempts to arouse a sense of
guilt in him as she chides him about the health and general disposition of their daughter. She poignantly expresses her continuing sorrow
over the death of Fanny Blood:

I cannot, without a thrill of delight, recollect views I have seen, which
are not to be forgotten—nor looks I have felt in every nerve which I shall
never more meet. The grave has closed over a dear friend, the friend of
my youth; still she is present with me, and I hear her soft voice warbling
as I stray over the heath. Fate has separated me from another, the fire
of whose eyes, tempered by infantine tenderness, still warms my breast;

even when gazing on these tremendous cliffs, sublime emotions absorb my soul. And, smile not, if I add, that the rosy tint of morning reminds me of a suffusion, which will never more charm my senses, unless it reappears on the cheeks of my child. Her sweet blushes I may yet hide in my bosom, and she is still too young to ask why starts the tear, so near akin to pleasure and pain? I cannot write any more at present. (59)

As the journey nears its end, Wollstonecraft deals with Imlay differently, launching a subconscious attack against him in the guise of political comment. She denounces the male pursuit of wealth, especially by men of commerce, and mixes her denunciation with lofty warning—"Cassandra was not the only prophetess whose warning voice has been disregarded" (190). Wollstonecraft must know he will ignore any plea, by now the philandering Imlay has sought refuge elsewhere from her intensity.

Nature and Style

Nevertheless, Wollstonecraft triumphs. Indeed, the popularity of *Letters from Sweden* among her published works stems from the very fact that it lacks the self-righteous, sharp-edged moralistic quality that especially characterizes her educational works and didactic fiction. A colloquial, chatty, much more mellow tone infuses the letters and allows her more readily than in the *Vindications* to meander from one topic to another, breaking away occasionally for swift associations, only to close with a recapitulation and an affirmation. She interrupts herself at will when something diverts her or seizes her imagination. Rarely economical with words, she expands her thoughts, narrating her experiences as a traveler, moralist, political analyst, and social observer, as well as mother and lover.

Until 1795 Wollstonecraft scarcely wrote about nature, although it occupied a central spot in her Yorkshire and Welsh childhood days. Now she refers to this childhood, for the Scandinavian tour reminds her of these earlier affinities. For the first time in her nonfiction, Mary Wollstonecraft explicitly proclaims herself a lover of open spaces, of the countryside and the quiet it affords; she joyfully indulges in her sense of a special union with nature. Her natural powers of observation appear in the first chapter when she remarks on the "most picturesque bay I ever saw" (9), and the "sight of some heart's-ease that peeped through the rocks" (13), and finally on the rocks themselves, a feature of the northern terrain that recurs as a motif throughout. The rocks emerge almost as independent characters on the voyage. "Come no further," she has them "emphatically" command; and later, she says that "the rocks . . . partook of the general repose, and reclined more heavily on their foundation" (14, 16). In a manner that recalls Coleridge, Wollstonecraft moves associatively from contemplation of the rocks' tranquility to thoughts of her child, which in turn induce melancholy and another series of ideas. In a prose variant of Coleridge's "Frost at Midnight," which she names "The Beauty of the Northern Summer's Evening," she considers herself "still a part of a mighty whole, from which I could not sever myself" (17)—ironic in the light of her recent suicidal history. Idyllic scenes of nature help Wollstonecraft forget unpleasant experiences in France and her personal trauma. They also foster a lilting, rhythmic poetic quality and feeling in her prose.

Rejoicing in the juniper, which appears as "the underwood of the forest" that leaves "images in the memory which the imagination will ever hold dear" (58), she foreshadows Wordsworth's feelings and thoughts on the daffodils. At the same time, her strong relationship with nature elicits moving passages reminiscent of Cowper and Young, in which senses blend with natural elements:

Balmy were the slumbers, and soft the gales, that refreshed me, when I awoke to follow, with an eye vaguely curious, the white sails, as they turned the cliffs, or seemed to take shelter under the pines which covered the little islands that so gracefully rose to render the terrific ocean beautiful. The fishermen were calmly casting their nets; whilst the seagulls hovered over the unruffled deep. Everything seemed to harmonize into tranquility—even the mournful call of the bittern was in cadence with the tinkling bells on the necks of the cows, that, pacing slowly one after the other, along an inviting path in the vale below, were repairing to the cottages to be milked. With what ineffable pleasure have I not gazed— and gazed again, losing my breath through my eyes—my very soul diffused itself in the scene—and, seeming to become all senses, glided in the scarcely agitated waves, melted in the freshening breeze. (73-74)

She recalls later that the most "genial and humane" people she knows feel intimate with nature, as nature wholesomely inspires Wollstonecraft herself. By contrast, the commerce-engrossed Imlay stands apart

from it. Although the repetitious sight of pines and fir groves gradually fatigues her, the evening appearance of the trees seems "better
calculated to produce poetical images. Passing through them, I have
been struck with a mystic kind of reverence, and I did, as it were,
homage to their venerable shadows" (85). Solitude, she avers, un-
leashes imagination.

Her body also benefits from nature. She becomes energized, delights
in a restored constitution, and takes the natural waters, sensibly con-
cluding that the advantage accrues not so much from their medicinal
qualities as from the air, the exercise, and the change of scenery
associated with them.

Repeatedly, however, she reverts to the idea that nature can unconsciously betray her. At times when its contemplation evokes sentiments she holds dear, recent memories suddenly sadden her. Nature
both intoxicates and depresses Wollstonecraft, adding a new, strong
dimension to the known facts of her life. Her intense love of it
borders on a mystically based passion and echoes the total submersion
in God recommended in the preface and prayers of *The Female
Reader* and in other earlier writings, but lost in the two *Vindications*.
Although she walks out of philosophical step with her century in
terms of her feminist ideas, in other respects her thinking echoes that
of her contemporaries. Based on this apprehension of nature, she
sometimes replaces the rationalist concepts of the pricean school with
others more akin to revelation or mystical experience. Her recognition
that nature incites the imagination and bestows life-giving properties
into which all are called and enfolded parallels a similar recognition
of Wordsworth and Coleridge.

Wollstonecraft's desire to capture the grandeur of nature leads to
sensitive prose, such as the following passage where, in a melancholic
mood, she presents an idea that amounts to a muted wish for death
expressed in symbolic terms. The language of "wings of thought"
notably recalls the language of earlier female mystics.[8]

...The gay cobweb-like appearance of the aged pines is a much finer
image of decay; the fibres whitening as they lose their moisture, imprisoned life seems to be stealing away. I cannot tell why—but death,
under every form, appears to me like something getting free—to expand
in I know not what element; nay I feel that this conscious being must
be as unfettered, have the wings of thought, before it can be happy. (132)

Her meditation on the relationship between nature and death also recalls the eighteenth-century literature of melancholy while the intensity of her feelings for nature cause her preoccupying dejection about Imlay to surface. She reevokes her earlier sense of God, but where previously she received comfort by praying to him (who had caused her melancholy), she now discovers the source or inspiration of these feelings to be nature:

Nature is the nurse of sentiment,—the true source of taste;—yet what misery, as well as rapture, is produced by a quick perception of the beautiful and sublime, when it is exercised in observing animated nature, when every beauteous feeling and emotion excites responsive sympathy, and the harmonized soul sinks into melancholy, or rises to extasy, just as the chords are touched, like the aeolian harp agitated by the changing wind. (58)

Sweden, Norway, and Denmark

As Wollstonecraft travels, she reacts to the characteristics of each country. In Denmark she becomes less preoccupied with nature, because she can "see" less as she thinks more frequently of her return to England. Apprehending Imlay's preference to hear about people and events rather than natural phenomena (surely an odd preference for the author of a book on topography), she defers to his wishes. "Enough, you will say, of inanimate nature, and of brutes," she predicts, "let me hear something of the inhabitants" (77). Her discovery that many bourgeois Swedes seem polite only in form causes her to prefer the company of unaffected peasants who personify hospitality. Alive to class distinctions, Wollstonecraft seems to be suggesting that the less affluent cannot afford the luxury of empty form.

She portrays the protracted affair of dining in Sweden in a style that highlights her distaste: dish upon dish is heaped together in an unappetizing fashion. To nullify the experience, she abruptly switches the subject to nature by musing on which season could provide sustenance for such excessive indulgence.

After denouncing drinking as an undesired social activity, Wollstonecraft launches an attack on attitudes toward servants, having finally abandoned her earlier negative view of them as cunning, almost childlike people who must be kept in place as a matter of course. Where before she had unthinkingly imitated traditionally snobbish attitudes, she now thoroughly embraces the *idea* of "equality" for all, although she persistently undercuts this analysis by treating education as a middle-class phenomenon and assuming the petty bourgeois should have servants. Sympathetic to their oppressed condition, she excuses servants' thieving on the grounds that they are "tantalized by seeing and preparing the dainties of which they are not to partake" (27). She condemns this differential treatment by referring to the effects of war and taxes that fall most heavily on the shoulders of the poor, commenting at length on the relationship between their poverty and ignorance, which affects the health of their overprotectively bundled-up children. More affluent Swedish women spoil their appearance by growing fat from indolence and lack of dietary care. Among all classes of women in the country, she notices that "their dress shows that vanity is more inherent than taste" (35). In her final diagnosis, Wollstonecraft finds the narrow intellectual range of the Swedes displeasing and ultimately intolerable, and the odor of rotting herring ruins any potential pleasure in the scenery.

Fortunately, she finds Norway much more to her taste than Sweden: "The Norwegians are more industrious and more opulent" (48). The political rule under which "the Norwegians appear to enjoy all the blessings of freedom" also appeals to her political philosophy.[9] As a case in point, she so admires their distribution of landed property into small farms that she calls Norway "the most free community I have ever observed" (61) (she had advocated this kind of society in *The Rights of Men*). In her historical imagination Wollstonecraft locates them poised on the brink of "the epoch which precedes the introduction of the arts and sciences."

She speaks with approval of the Norwegian prince royal, who, acting in consort with Count Bernstorff, the Danish prime minister, is responsible for substantial reforms and laws. She pronounces the people of Denmark and Norway "the least oppressed people of Europe. The press is free. They translate any of the French publications of the day, [and] deliver their opinion . . . without fearing to displease the government" (66-67).

When the matter of women, diet, and drink arises, Wollstonecraft's inclination for Norway over Sweden leads to an interesting discrepancy. Although she mentions activities similar to those she observed in Sweden (the length of meals, the treatment of servants, women's vanity), she treats these customs in Norway much more casually.

Three or four short paragraphs suffice because her attraction to Norway's better qualities induce her to underplay its less positive aspects. In some respects the third country she visits, Denmark, fares even worse than Sweden. She brands the well-to-do Danes as indolent (surely a strange word in this context), when she narrates the story of a fire during which the rich retrieved their own possessions instead of trying to save thousands of poorer homes: "This kind of indolence, respecting what does not immediately concern them, seems to characterize the Danes" (151).[10]

She starts formulating her attitude toward Denmark during her trip from Tonsberg to Laurvig where she notes almost immediately the change in people's manners, "more cunning and fraudulent as I advance towards the westward" (95). Even Swedish prices are lower. Upon arrival in Denmark, she offers her first impressions: "If I say that the houses did not disgust me, I tell you all I remember of them; for I cannot recollect any pleasurable sensations they excited; or that any object produced by nature or art, took me out of myself" (168).

For Count Bernstorff, as for Norway's reforming prince royal, she reserves an unusual degree of praise—"the wisest of ministers" she concludes (152). But even Count Bernstorff cannot alter the image of Danish complacency, which Wollstonecraft calls the "stagnant state of the public mind." She attributes an excess of sensuality to this laziness. In Copenhagen, she comments on "the gross debaucheries into which the lower order of people fall, and the promiscuous amours of the men of the middling class with their female servants" (159). She concludes that intoxication, a popular vice in England as well as the northern states of Europe, constitutes the "greatest impediment to the world's improvement" (163). She reserves her major dissatisfaction with Denmark for the diminishing practice of vassalage, which prevents the Danes from having the "sprightly gait of the Norwegians" (158). She calls for the dissolution of this remnant of feudalism, for in the wake of its disappearance "that sordid avarice which every modification of slavery is calculated to produce" (159) will also cease.

Everything considered, Norway is her favorite country, perhaps the result of a political comparison, or from her longer stay in that country; certainly the supplementary notes support the former view. Part 1 of the supplement offers ethnographical and topographical descriptions of Norway; Part 2 mentions the redistribution of wealth that is an important element in her political perspective. Since she condemns the pursuit of wealth, pride in rank, and unequal class relationships, national attempts to cope positively with these problems influence her judgments. Politically, moreover, Wollstonecraft's sympathies would be more likely to lie with Denmark-ruled Norway, especially since, under the influence of enlightenment and French revolutionary ideas, Norway sought equality with Denmark. (It is worth noting that it is often difficult to fit Wollstonecraft's observations with her political ideas, since she now criticizes republican France while praising colonial Norway.)

Politics and People

By 1795 Mary Wollstonecraft has developed a strong political consciousness born of a combination of wide reading, social intercourse, and her own experiences. Her sense of self and her emotional security developed less surely. Her love for her daughter and for the peace and beauty of nature, and her insatiable absorption in the human condition claim her attention in largely equal parts. A consuming interest in educational matters, in crime and its motivation, and in prisons and prisoners also informs her political analysis.

Four paragraphs into the first letter, Wollstonecraft presents the reader with an example of her political outlook in her picture of two systems. In one system people work for themselves and therefore have something to gain from their labors, and in the other what she calls despotism inherently oppresses the workers or vassals. "Despotism, as is usually the case," she says of the latter, "I found had here cramped the industry of man. The pilots being paid by the king, and scantily, they will not run into any danger, or even quit their hovels, if they can possibly avoid it, only to fulfill what is termed their duty. How different, is it on the English coast, where, in the most stormy weather, boats immediately hail you, brought out by the expectation of extraordinary profit" (8). She mentions the "cloven foot of despotism" (121), but as the letters continue she begins to condemn the tyranny of wealth as "still more galling and debasing than that of rank," and by letter XVII she is denouncing businessmen as "domestic tyrants, coldly immersed in their own affairs" (151). (This is a fine example not only of Wollstonecraft's capacity to generalize, the businessman Imlay being the particular spur

to her thought, but of the lack of diplomacy induced by her passionate nature.) In letter XXII her tone has become sharply resent-
ful as she equates men of commerce with cunning priests and dishonest
statesmen: "Men entirely devoted to commerce never acquire, or lose,
all taste and greatness of mind. An ostentatious display of wealth
without elegance, and a greedy enjoyment of pleasure without sentiment, embrutes them till they term all virtue, of an heroic cast, romantic attempts of something above our nature; and anxiety about the
welfare of others, a search after misery, in which we have no concern"
(187). She takes time to explain her attitude toward merchants: "I
was led into these reflections when I heard of some tricks practiced
by merchants, miscalled reputable, and certainly men of property,
during the present war" (120). Indeed, she heaps such wholesale contempt on businessmen "so ignorant of the state of other countries,
that they dogmatically assert that Denmark is the happiest country
in the world" (151) that at times she appears to use her writing to
embarrass or reprimand Imlay in public.

Wherever she goes, she scrutinizes the condition of women, whether
mothers, daughters, wives, servants, old women, hostesses, or children.
Echoing *The Rights of Women*, she terms women of the merchant
class, "simple notable housewives, without accomplishments, or any
of the charms that adorn more advanced social life" (152). Although
consistently attuned to the role of women and preeminently to their
lack of power, she usually tags as male-inspired the motor force behind the occasional desire for power exemplified in competition,
avarice, and selfishness. She censures female attention to social niceties
and to the trappings of its accompanying sloth as harshly as she
condemns commerce.

She alternately praises and upbraids women individually and as
representatives of their roles or positions. The moving story of Matilda,
George III's sister, who was married at fifteen by proxy to the deranged
(because abused) Christian VII and died at twenty-four, totally en-
gages Wollstonecraft's sympathies despite her high rank. While denouncing Matilda's victimization at the hands of the crazed king,
Wollstonecraft refrains from judging her obvious adultery with
Struensee, the court physician who held the king in his power.[11] "Be
that as it may [adultery or not,]" argues Wollstonecraft, "she certainly
was not a woman of gallantry; and if she had an attachment for him,
it did not disgrace her heart or understanding, the king being a

notorious debauchess [sic]; and an idiot into the bargain" (153-54). Wollstonecraft's private moral standards reflect her public ones.[12]

Other women fare less well in her estimation. Ignorant mothers especially disappoint her because they directly affect a vitally significant area of her life—the education of children. She upbraids them now as she did in her early educational works and in *The Rights of Woman*. In numerous letters she comments on the condition of children, how they are reared, the unhealthiness of excessive clothing, their diet, and the harm that ill-educated mothers cause: "The children are spoilt . . . when left to the care of weak, indulgent mothers, who, having no principle of action to regulate their feelings, become the slaves of infants, enfeebling both body and mind by false tenderness" (152).

Speaking of women servants, she castigates the practice of passing on the most menial, laborious tasks "to those poor drudges." "In the winter," she asserts, "I am told, they take the linen down to the river, to wash it in the cold water; and though their hands, cut by ice, are cracked and bleeding, the men, their fellow servants, will not disgrace their manhood by carrying a tub to lighten their burden" (26). Despite her championship of these women, Wollstonecraft never hints that the existence of such a class as servants politically troubles her: "We must have our servants," she proclaims. This sharp contradiction between her defense of the poor and her acceptance of class distinctions had begun to blunt by 1797. Wollstonecraft's moral pen-lashing at this time, however, extends beyond women. Aghast at the drinking habits of the Scandinavians, she allows her personal preferences to surface; devoid of sympathy for the solace the cold and poverty-stricken might find in alcohol, she sneers at the "churlish pleasure of drinking drams" (25).

On her return from Gothenburg to pick up her daughter, she arrives at Moss where even beauty and a decent standard of living for villagers cannot stanch her complaints about the ways in which military service affects Norwegians. At Christiania (Oslo), she condemns commerce and tyranny in the shape of the grand bailiffs who are rooted in the Danish aristocracy. Also, Scandinavia generally receives a poor rating on intellectual grounds: "I should not like to live continually in the country, with people whose minds have such a narrow range. My heart would frequently be interested; but my mind would languish for more companionable society" (41).

Wollstonecraft prefers Norway politically to the other Scandinavian countries because people receive better care despite the fact that it comes from a royal (albeit benevolent) despot. She seems able to temper her hatred of arbitrary rank when it is used in the service of the general population, but she does not forget the class relationship of power. In modern parlance it is a reformist position: "Though the Norwegians are not in the abject state of the Irish, yet this second-hand government is still felt . . . to benefit the domineering [i.e., colonial] state" (121).

In the last lap of the journey to Hamburg, Wollstonecraft offers a final word on the recurring theme of moral character. She concludes that men's "whole system of morality is in general held together by one grand principle, which loses its force . . . in the chase after wealth. . . . To business, as it is termed, everything must give way. . . . Profit and profit [sic] are the only speculations" (190-91). Behind all great affairs to which she has been privy there lurks nothing but "mean machinery."[13]

Not until she reaches Hamburg does she attempt a synthesis of her contrasting impressions. "Nothing can be stronger," she observes,

than the contrast which this flat country and strand afford, compared with the mountains, and rocky coast, I have lately dwelt so much among. In fancy I return to a favourite spot, where I seemed to have retired from man and wretchedness; but the din of trade drags me back to all the care I left behind, when lost in sublime emotions. Rocks aspiring towards the heavens, and as it were, shutting out sorrow, surrounded me, whilst peace appeared to steal along the lake to calm my bosom, modulating the wind that agitated the neighbouring poplars. Now I hear only an account of the tricks of trade, or listen to the distressful tale of some victim of ambition. (192)

She has reentered the world, wistfully remarking in her final paragraph that "My spirit of observation seems to have fled" (196).

Throughout the work Wollstonecraft strikes the armchair reader as considerably more than a traveler venturing to describe unknown lands, since she introduces such rich experiences to the narrative. That she was a woman making a journey with only a female servant and an infant daughter might seem the most amazing adventure of all. She expresses concern for the welfare of strangers down to matters of diet and wet nursing. Her avowed aim to "trace the progress of the world's improvement" (letter XIX) provokes a continual comparison of the three Scandinavian countries with Germany. She nurtures a special regard for people on the edge of survival; the plight of servants, whose lot is tantamount to slavery, horrifies her. But again she singles women out: "The men stand up for the dignity of men, by oppressing the women" (26).

Wollstonecraft's poignant struggle is revealed in the contrast she draws between her atypical carpe diem approach ("Let me catch pleasure on the wing—I may be melancholy tomorrow," 100) and her indulgence in grief: "At present black melancholy hovers round my footsteps; and sorrow sheds a mildew over all the future prospects, which hope no longer gilds" (117). Despairing, she confides, "In this city, thoughtfulness seemed to be sliding into melancholy. . . . I felt like a bird fluttering on the ground unable to mount; yet unwilling to crawl tranquilly like a reptile" (121-22).[14] Yet the sentence concludes on an optimistic note that propels her "like a reptile, whilst still conscious it had wings." Immediately, she acts to dissolve the fog that threatens to cloud her mind: "I walked out, for the open air is always my remedy when an aching head proceeds from an oppressed heart" (122). "The sight of the slaves" immediately strikes her and her emotions come full circle.

As an index to her independent nature, her aesthetic sense, and her political insight, *Letters from Sweden* still draws readers after almost two centuries. Its enduring strength flows from these elements combined with the art and unity of its framing devices, its singular (for her and for women writers) journey motif, its transcendent melancholy, and raw emotion. As Godwin correctly observed, "She speaks of her sorrows, in a way that fills us with melancholy, and dissolves us in tenderness, at the same time that she displays a genius which commands all our admiration."[15]

Chapter Eight

The Wrongs of
Woman, or Maria:
A Fictional Vindication

Historical and Literary Background

Wollstonecraft attempted a new work of didactic fiction that would address a wide range of sociopolitical, legal, and economic abuses. Having seen the streets of Paris flowing with blood and risked the moral censure of the world in her private and public life, she was undeterred by the fact that times were dangerous for radicals. In fact, the momentum of the decade propelled radicals toward opinion fiction and caused them to reassess every form of injustice. This impetus came in part from the growing market for such works and the liberalizing of ideas fostered by the French Revolution. Thus her ideas were more accessible and gave her an avenue to explore the question of human fulfillment that preoccupied her.[1] At the same time, having simultaneously tried to piece together and evaluate the historical process in *The French Revolution*, Wollstonecraft planned to sketch a more personal fictional moral history of herself and of women in general. In addition, a successful relationship with William Godwin inspired her to turn again to fiction.

Just as *Mary, A Fiction* helped to assuage her grief for the death of Fanny Blood, so *The Wrongs of Woman* enabled her to vent her anger at Imlay's behavior and secondarily at her brother-in-law's treatment of her sister Eliza. She moved in circles with an abundance of publicly successful "fiction-mentors" from William Godwin and Thomas Holcroft to Charlotte Smith and Elizabeth Inchbald. Their polemical fiction appealed to Wollstonecraft's stylistic temperament and rigorous sense of justice, while the popularity of the roman à thèse guaranteed her a respectable fictional subgenre for her work. In 1788 when she wrote *Mary, A Fiction*, her purpose was to examine a young woman's consciousness and its impact on individuals and the world. This time she aimed higher and wider to investigate the social and political consciousness of the age and its effect on women. Rather than locating the perspective of the novel in an individual's consciousness, she was bent on probing the complex dialectic created by that consciousness in its contact with the world. The public and private, the worldly and domestic, objective data and subjective response no longer seemed to be separable. She also intended to work out aspects of her personal life in the story of Darnford and Maria, and of her evolving ideology in the story of a laboring woman's doubly jeopardized struggle to survive.

She wrote herself and her experiences into the narrative of *Thoughts* with her ideas about child rearing, education, and middle- and upper-class female pastimes and occupations. Her persona was evident also in *Mary, A Fiction* in its exploration of a moral-sentimental educacation and in the two *Vindications* with her anger against oppression and injustice. *Letters from Sweden* was made up of her political commentary and perspectives on the everyday lives of men and women. The *Wrongs of Woman* was no different, and in addition was potentially the second part of both *Mary, A Fiction* and *A Vindication of the Rights of Woman*, as Wollstonecraft demonstrated her indignation at the treatment accorded women plus an implicit political critique and a call for resistance.

Wollstonecraft's reading material and possible indirect influences at the time included *Memoirs of Emma Courtney* (1796) by Mary Hays, which both she and William Godwin had read in manuscript; possibly *A Simple Story* (1791) and *Nature and Art* (1796), both by Elizabeth Inchbald; *Anna St. Ives* (1792) by Thomas Holcroft, in which a resourceful, outspoken, female militant wards off a rake-seducer; *Caleb Williams* by William Godwin, which Wollstonecraft borrowed from Godwin in 1796 and 1797; and *Desmond* (1792) and *The Old Manor House* (1793) by Charlotte Smith. In the last two, Smith, in addition to exposing aspects of her difficult circumstances, argued against the subjugation of women by sociosexual convention and other social injustices.[2] *The Sorrows of Young Werther* by Wolfgang von Goethe (translated into English in 1779), and *La Nouvelle Héloïse* by Jean-Jacques Rousseau (first London edition

1784) had helped to shape her treatment of feelings in fiction. By the early 1790s, however, and certainly by 1797, she had come to regard feelings much more as a trap than she had in *Mary, A Fiction*. Wollstonecraft fused three case histories by means of a go-between character, a laboring woman who brings the lovers together. She used three principal sources for her material. First, there were her own experiences with Imlay and her family. In addition, there was information culled from her visit to Bedlam in 1797 with Godwin and Johnson and from her interest in asylums stemming from the possible madness of her brother Henry. Finally, she was influenced by the innumerable books of social and political commentary, as well as works of fiction and culture, that she reviewed for the *Analytical Review* when she resumed her job there in 1796.[3] The idea of integrated case histories was present in William Godwin's fiction, where he explored his studies of character in great psychological detail. *Mary, A Fiction* had shown that Wollstonecraft also had a talent for this fictional form, which enabled her to provide psychological portraits as well as political commentary in great variety and depth.

Organization, Style, and Ideas

Because of personal experiences, Mary Wollstonecraft publicized the plight of people in all forms of slavery by depicting the independently minded at odds with bourgeois society. In *The Wrongs of Woman* she hammered as usual at the specific bondage of women, bringing people she had known into a cluster of situations she had observed or experienced.[4] She drew women of all classes who were physically and psychologically manacled in marriage, from husbands and lovers who mistreat women to mistresses, wives, daughters, prostitutes, and laboring women who suffer at the hands of men. She showed their degradation in a variety of institutional settings from asylums to hospitals and courts. The inadequacy of female education across class lines also featured prominently. Echoing a major battle in Wollstonecraft's life, reason and emotion fought for control throughout this novel.

A dramatically conceived context frames her ideas. Jemima, an asylum warden, tends Maria, who is legally incarcerated there by her husband. Maria meets Henry Darnford, another unjustly held inmate, who narrates the story of his confinement. Although backstage for most of the novel, Darnford shapes the action significantly, while his personal account serves the currently popular vogue for tales of adventure set in the United States.[5] To explain her own dire straits, Maria permits Darnford to read the memoirs she has recorded for her kidnapped daughter—a modified, truncated version of Wollstonecraft's *Mary, A Fiction*. A warm intimacy develops between the two, and they become lovers. Their relationship encourages Jemima to share with them her suppressed emotions and troubles. Thus we see Wollstonecraft's structural attempt to present each character in the round.

The story is roughly divided into three sections, each a tale within a tale. (This was a common device employed by almost all of the earlier women novelists, such as Sarah Fielding in *The Governess*, Sarah Scott in *Millenium Hall*, and Eliza Haywood in *The British Recluse*.) The first four chapters detail Maria's captive situation, her friendship with Jemima, and Darnford's narrative. Chapter 5, twice the length of any other chapter, outlines Jemima's life history. Chapters 7 through 14 consist of Maria's memoirs to her child, in fact, a pretext to recount her own history. The remainder of the novel is made up of three chapters and a conclusion, which are described by Godwin as "broken paragraphs and half-finished sentences." These fragments give rise to speculation about Wollstonecraft's possible final version and her philosophical and emotional uncertainties. Godwin wrote an appendix, which he inserted as an apologia for her seeming indecision. He claimed that the first fifteen chapters were meant to form Part 1 of a larger opus.

These broken paragraphs continue the individual stories in various forms while the alternative endings suggest that Darnford has been unfaithful and that Maria has miscarried their child. The passage superscribed "The End" reads as a possible sequel in which a lonely Maria is dissuaded from suicide by Jemima. Maria must live for her daughter's benefit if not for her own, so that the child will not be forced to experience the misery of Jemima's motherless upbringing. (We assume Maria's eventual release.)

Although Wollstonecraft's overall plan for the work remains impossible to discern, she clearly states her aim and subject in the introduction: "[Matrimonial despotism of heart and conduct] appear to me to be the peculiar Wrongs of Woman, because they degrade the mind. What are termed great misfortunes, may more forcibly impress the mind of common readers; they have more of what may justly be termed *stage effect*; but it is the delineation of finer sensations, which, in my opinion, constitutes the merit of our best novels. This is what I have in view; and to show the wrongs of different classes of women, equally oppressive, though, from the differences of education, necessarily various" (8).

William Godwin's final remarks to the reader complete Wollstonecraft's statement of purpose: "It was particularly the design of the author, in the present instance, to make her story subordinate to a great moral purpose, that of exhibiting the misery and oppression, peculiar to women, that arise out of the partial laws and customs of society.— This view restrained her fancy. It was necessary for her, to place in a striking point of view, evils that are too frequently overlooked, and to drag into light those details of oppression, of which the grosser and more insensible part of mankind make little account" (154). Wollstonecraft, in short, intended to write a didactic novel with a purposeful aesthetic dimension that would enhance her ideas. Her subject was the injustice suffered by women as a whole, with particular attention to the legally sanctioned control of their lives through marriage, the lot of single women, and the physical, psychological, and sociopolitical abuse of working people.

Maria as Independent Hero: A Decade Later

As the book opens, the manacled Maria sits on center stage, principal character and putative major victim. From a feminist perspective, the scene graphically represents the opening lines of Rousseau's *Social Contract*, showing women characters who live literally imprisoned lives. Over a period of time Maria develops a rapprochement with the servant Jemima, who fosters a relationship between Maria and Darnford. Maria trusts Darnford to read her memoirs, a version of the popular tracts on the theme of a "Mother's Advice to Daughters."[6] An established setting ("born in one of the most romantic parts of England," 75) and a detailed family background ("My father had been a captain of a man of war . . . my eldest brother . . . became in due form the deputy-tyrant of the house . . . my mother had an indolence of character," 75-76), combines standard fare with such inimitably wollstonecraftian elements as the attack on primogeniture. Maria's sole friend and mentor, an uncle who instructs her in the principles of liberal education, unintentionally burdens her with future misery by bribing the son of a neighboring merchant to marry her. Because her mother dies and her suitor, George Venables, misrepresents himself as an altruistic young man, Maria consents to a marriage.

The situation rapidly deteriorates. George drinks, whores, gambles, and ultimately tries to "sell" Maria's "favors" to a friend, a move she adamantly resists by abandoning her husband. She undertakes the separation with full knowledge of the consequences, especially the inequities of the laws against women. Her money and her child legally belong to her husband who, short of murdering her, can treat her as he chooses.[7] Like other eighteenth-century wives, Maria becomes his captive and his property—until Wollstonecraft shifts the action into another gear.

Maria shares with Mary, the protagonist of Wollstonecraft's first novel, the fact that each is married for her money, in the former case to gain inherited wealth, in the latter to unite two estates. Mary's situation shows how power continued to depend on the possession of landed wealth, while Maria's exposes the inequity of inheritance laws that rendered husbands sole possessors of women's money. Maria rebels altogether rejects Venables in her mind, escapes, and is eventually hunted down like an animal. Venables executes a ruthless plan as he attempts to retrieve his lost "property," but Maria stands firm. When Venables sues her for adultery, she confronts the judge, harangues the jury, and delivers the best short political speech in the early English novel on behalf of female equality.[8] But like Mary, she is caught in her own sensibility, struggling to avoid not only the image of the silly female but the often woman-created literary one of the lady of sensibility, an image that frequently attracted and overwhelmed Wollstonecraft herself.[9]

Jemima

Jemima's story in *The Wrongs of Woman* highlights Wollstonecraft's developing analysis of class divisions within society. From the *Rights of Woman* in 1790 to her recent travels throughout Scandinavia, she had been reevaluating her thoughts on that subject; in her earliest works she was negative about servants, depicting them as cunning plotters to be thwarted, and poor people as needy recipients of Christian charity. Her remarks about servants in *Thoughts*, and in *Original Stories* her treatment of crazy Robin, the impoverished schoolteacher, and the exigent shopkeeper display her point of view. Even the two *Vindications*, which address economic privilege and class tyranny, concentrate on the relief of middle-class women.

By the time Wollstonecraft wrote *The Wrongs of Woman*, however, several influences had irreversibly affected her thinking and helped shape her new fiction. These included political thinkers and the circumstances of the French Revolution; her experiences abroad and her own reading; her exposure to the lot of servants, sailors, prostitutes, prisoners, and soldiers; and other injustices, many of which she witnessed at first hand. As a result, the tale from beginning to end indicts society, as women's social conditioning, their social (lack of) possibilities, and their inability to work for a decent living reappear in a reformulation of the laboring class. Jemima, the daughter of servants, [is] "left in dirt, to cry with cold and hunger" (53) when her mother dies. Prematurely old from neglect, beaten without mercy, a drudge for maids, apprentices, and children, Jemima steals to eat. At the age of sixteen, tall and presentable, she attracts the master (a friend of her stepmother), to whom she is bound as apprentice. She becomes pregnant by him, is discovered, and turned out into the street where she begs and prostitutes herself. After entering service, she is duped out of her earnings. Finally she takes to washing clothes, but fails to obtain necessary medical treatment on account of her poverty, and winds up in a workhouse where the overseer observes "something resolute in my manner" (69), and gives Jemima her present job as an asylum warden.

Wollstonecraft makes this unrelieved tale of abuse and rejection effective by placing it between the narratives of Maria and Darnford where it serves as a foil to both. Their relatively privileged and comfortable lives underscore the exigencies of Jemima's existence. No recourse but charity remains. No let-up, no escape exists, as middle-class alternatives lie beyond her reach. However psychologically and even physically uncomfortable it may be, Maria, like Wollstonecraft and Eliza, can afford to escape in a coach, shelter in a boarding house, write for help, and trade on demeanor and gentility. Darnford can hire lawyers and sue. But penniless Jemima must work hard and persevere, salt away whatever she can, curb her own emotions, and harden herself to stay alive. Her story illuminates the situation facing the eighteenth-century poor in much the same way as Charles Dickens and Henry Mayhew expose the harsh realities of poverty in the nineteenth century.[10]

Also to the point, Wollstonecraft seems to be the first to present in the same work the difficulties faced by women of different classes. For example, despite the fact that Moll Flanders, Roxana, Pamela, and Clarissa predate Jemima and Maria, Daniel Defoe and Samuel Richardson do not knit their lives together into the texture of the same work; Wollstonecraft, on the contrary, appears to recognize the political and dramatic significance of illustrating class differences through major female characters side by side in the same work.

Moreover, what Wollstonecraft suggests and her story dramatizes is the plight of a woman informally and callously shaped or, in a loose sense, educated by the world, who develops a strong will as a result. She constantly stresses Jemima's determination to the point at which persistence and struggle against injustice seem to be in themselves the methods by which Jemima endeavors to overcome and even alter her situation. In more general terms, Wollstonecraft seems to be saying that an individual, from whatever class, has an internal, events-motivated power that can bring about or at least allow for the possibility of personal, if not economic, autonomy. Because of her own will and its effect on her experiences, Wollstonecraft never seems to lose sight of the view that individual strength counts as a critical factor in any effort to subdue inequities. (This in part contributed to her great despair over Imlay, for she refused to give in and chose suicide over surrender.)

A further resemblance between Wollstonecraft and her characters lies in the fact that Maria and Jemima argue a philosophy that they embody in practice. Despite their treatment as soiled goods in a society of commerce, they avoid death and stand firm. As Maria contemplates her situation and rebels, Jemima copes within her capacity. Their lives oppose those of the more passive, walk-on characters—the sailor's wife, the haberdasher's wife, the landlady, their mothers, and others. Wollstonecraft resolves Richardson's moral impasse in *Pamela* (how can a woman succeed and not become a kept woman in the end?) by proposing staying power and struggle as answers.

The sharp class differences between Maria and Jemima belie their surprising similarities. Physically and psychologically mangled, emptied of self-love, society has imprisoned both. Maria finally opts within her role and position as a mother to live for her child, while Jemima, servantlike, resolves to live for her new mistress, Maria, and the child. More important yet unstated, both decide to live for themselves, because their altruism has endowed their lives with new meaning. In one of several posited endings, Wollstonecraft transforms the historical dependence of women into a strength. Here the triangle of bonding with Maria, Jemima, and the child reflects a female variant on the Mary-Henry-Henry's mother triangle in *Mary, A Fiction*. Now, however, a healthy child, fictional Fanny Imlay, replaces a somewhat romantically ailing hero, while two vigorous women take over from romantic Mary and an ethereal mother. As a strong vision of class as well as gender alliance, the outcome appears as sophisticated a political message as any in the eighteenth-century novel.

Maria averts death by a selfless response to the plight of women and the new faith in herself that assertive thinking engenders. Rejecting suicide because of this newly discovered self-realization (a key factor in Wollstonecraft's educational ideas), Maria emerges as an important fictional foremother in the battle for women's freedom. As the working hero who casts her lot with another oppressed woman, Jemima, in one ending, appears to tower as the hope of the future, a latter-day dea ex machina who saves the child to save the future.

On the other hand, the suggested endings in which Jemima is spotlighted as the savior of both the child and Maria *still* depict her as a servant. Whether Mary Wollstonecraft would have worked out the dramatic symbolism of the fragments—that the heroic laboring woman saves the future and womankind—can never be ascertained, for she told a friend that she had not yet begun, as she says, "to adjust my events into a story, the outline of which I had sketched in my mind at the commencement."[11] More likely, in view of Wollstonecraft's position on middle-class women, Jemima could have been saving the child and Maria so that Maria could, contrary to the pull of feelings, act as the trio's motive force and leader. Evidence for the latter perspective is manifest in the fact of saving Maria, which points to her future center-stage heroism. (The title indicates this, too.) The idea that Wollstonecraft would ultimately not have shown Jemima as the major protagonist is equally well corroborated by the contemporaneous *Letters on the Management of Infants* in which she argues the importance of the example of middle-class women: "My advice will probably be found most useful to mothers in the middle class; and it is from them that the lower imperceptibly gains improvement. Custom, produced by reason, in one, may safely be the effect of imitation in the other."[12]

Autobiographical Elements

If *The Wrongs of Woman* etches the strife and strivings of women in general, it also obliquely defends the actions of Eliza and Mary Wollstonecraft, especially Eliza's escape from Meredith Bishop and abandonment of her child. Perhaps seeking to justify her own actions in January 1783, Wollstonecraft presents the events that precipitate Maria's escape as more than just cause for her flight, particularly when George Venables threatens to bring himself and Maria into a pimp-prostitute relationship by assuring his best friend in a letter that every woman, including Maria as his wifely property, has her price.

Distraught when she learns of Venables's indecent proposal, Maria executes her plan. The graphic first-person account of the coach ride reads as a variation of Wollstonecraft's letter to Everina when she engineered Eliza's escape. "I almost feared that the coach would break down before I got out of the street. . . . My mind, during the past few days, seemed, as it were, disengaged from my body; but, now the struggle was over, I felt very forcibly the effect which perturbation of spirits produced on a woman in my situation."[13] Wollstonecraft has recast Eliza's flight from her husband and conflated many other predicaments of her own and her sister's.

Earlier, Wollstonecraft had sketched the situation they faced as governesses, a form of employment that she characterized as "the only one in which even a well-educated woman, with more than ordinary talents, can struggle for a subsistence; and even this is a dependence next to menial" (96). The younger sister's death thus depicted in *The Wrongs of Woman* might be an elder sister's fictional tribute to the living Eliza's courage and stamina. In Maria's assertion that the younger sister showed "false pride" when she "shrunk at the name of Milliner or Mantuaworker as degrading to a gentlewoman" (96), Wollstonecraft reaffirms her respectful understanding of women who work at arduous, thankless jobs.

Apart from Maria's own family, who strikingly resemble Wollstonecraft's, the most familiar character is Henry Darnford, suggested by Gilbert Imlay. Maria's love for Henry stands as an autobiographical key to Wollstonecraft's passionate devotion to Imlay. Before his initial entrance, the women know something of Darnford's education and sophistication. In his collection of books (which includes Dryden, Milton, and Rousseau, with whom Wollstonecraft was so often involved in her writing), "there was a fragment, containing various observations on the present state of society and government, with a comparative view of the politics of Europe and America. These remarks were written with a degree of generous warmth, when alluding to the enslaved state of the labouring majority, perfectly in unison with Maria's mode of thinking" (36). Again Wollstonecraft stresses class as she praises Imlay's writings and hints at the possible influence of North American thinking on her new understanding.

Darnford's accomplishments and personal attractiveness appeal to Maria's "wayward heart," for she has never learned to restrain her natural impulses. In this daughter of sentiment, head and heart are opposed, as they are in *Mary, A Fiction* and *The Rights of Woman*, but Maria's heart wins. This is a seeming indictment by the now detached Wollstonecraft of her own relationship with Imlay, supported by the posited conclusion that shows Darnford's abandonment of Maria.

Unlike the stories of Maria and Jemima, Darnford's sounds as fragmented as Wollstonecraft's speculative conclusions. He remains a partially sympathetic character because he has tried to overcome his "womanizing" vice, and he conscientiously despises inequality of condition and commerce. A picture of the real and imagined Imlay springs to life, with all his positive qualities embodied in Darnford and his negative aspects caught—his fickleness and his preference for the ephemeral in personal relationships—in Darnford's absolved past sins. At the same time, the ending in which Darnford might abandon Maria indicates some measure of Wollstonecraft's continuing resentment.

These various conclusions chart Wollstonecraft's creative anxieties and uncertainty. On balance, however, if she is reshaping her experiences with Imlay, Darnford's desertion of Maria bespeaks a cad. In the book's terms, Maria's love for him is manifestly justified, not unlike Wollstonecraft's frustrated efforts to be on closer terms with Fuseli in 1791. In both cases, rejection breeds a kind of despair.

Possibly part of Jemima's psychological profile is modeled on the

French maid Marguerite, for whom Wollstonecraft felt a great devotion. (Marguerite, however, was probably very French and genteel.) Certainly Marguerite knew Wollstonecraft in her bleakest hours, from the time that Imlay was abandoning her until Wollstonecraft's death. Wollstonecraft might have transposed to Jemima her admiration for Marguerite (whom she trusted to the point of leaving her with her baby both on her Scandinavian voyage and when she tried to take her own life). In any event, Marguerite must have helped open Wollstonecraft's eyes to the difficulties of being a servant.

Political Features

The Wrongs of Woman is a long disquisition, a didactic fictional tract on the effect of environment, custom (including ideas about marriage and romantic love), and unjust laws on the lives of women. Jemima fights environment primarily, but not exclusively; Maria fights custom and law primarily, but not exclusively. If *The Rights of Woman* integrates Wollstonecraft's political theories, *The Wrongs of Woman* fits those theories into a practical context. It represents a fictional culmination for one who learned, most directly from the French Revolution, the interrelation of thoughts and deeds. Influenced by Godwin's critiques, which she earnestly sought, Wollstonecraft wrote this book, in his words, "slowly and with a mature consideration."[14] She sought to integrate her ideas on intellectual currents of thought propounded by the likes of Thomas Paine. Imprisonment and freedom, the rich and the poor, personal integrity and political vision, individualism and the common good comprised the essential elements. Wollstonecraft adapted the notion that every age and generation must be free to act for itself so that it became the motivation for her own idea that female emancipation was needed now.

The Wrongs of Woman possesses a hard edge to it, a bite and a personal intensity that are new to Wollstonecraft's writing. Where *The Cave of Fancy* failed utterly as an imaginative rendition of the correct means of educating females, the story of Jemima emerges triumphantly. Despite her generalized role as the spokeswoman for all females, Maria, too, claims an inimitable identity that is clinched in the court scene. Pursued and penalized for standing on her own feet, drugged and chained in a lunatic asylum for asserting her independence, Maria embodies the conflict between subjective vision and sociopolitical duty, and the quest for self-realization in which her feelings play her false while her intellect serves her well. Unlike *Mary, A Fiction* and *The Rights of Woman*, *The Wrongs of Woman* demystifies the paradoxes of Wollstonecraft's experience: romantic love, unhappy marriage, sensibility, and fierce passion now have fewer, if any, redeeming qualities.

In addition to her contribution to the debate between reason and feeling, Wollstonecraft deftly employs gothic elements by portraying dungeons, unearthly figures and cries, emotional excesses, an awesome scene of peril, a mysterious chase, and an ominous madhouse setting. Exciting action and melodrama bind the work together just as an emotional, constantly hovering tension between love and fear sustains it. Wollstonecraft even borrows from the gothic genre the central theme of the persecuted virtuous woman who flees the aggressive and dominating "sadist." As in *The Rights of Men*, however, she resolutely declares she is not using literary devices and tricks, while obviously employing them to good effect.

Wollstonecraft was the first woman to write a self-consciously political novel on behalf of women with the avowed intention of redressing their inequality. She tried to sharpen and broaden her perspective by showing wrongs perpetrated not just against women but against humanity in general. Originally intended to indict the particular wrongs of women, the novel reads as a revolutionary testament or early manifesto of democracy as it more widely indicts society, law, marriage, education, and aristocracy. She defined key problems through the weapon of her writing, but her final political solution rested within the system, consistent with her championship of the middle-class, the ultimate redeemers of the laboring poor, in their battle against the aristocracy. Furthermore, the radically flawed legal system of the eighteenth century that she conjures up cannot restore benefits hitherto denied Maria and Jemima.

In *The Wrongs of Woman* the will to struggle remains integral to the major characters' lives just as it did to Wollstonecraft on her deathbed. During her last lucid moments, she gasped out to Godwin the essence of her struggle—words that she might as easily have applied to Maria as she fought to leave the asylum or to all the wronged women, men, and children on whose behalf she had spent her adult life campaigning—"a struggle," she told him after a five-minute shivering fit, "between life and death."[15]

Chapter Nine

Mary Wollstonecraft: An Assessment

In Wollstonecraft's day, social and political England stood in dire need of change, symbolized by the struggle for Parliamentary reform. The newly industrialized commercial middle class was unrepresented in the House of Commons. Dissenters—Baptists, Presbyterians, and Independents alike—were excluded by the Test and Corporation Acts from holding any royal appointment in civil government or attending Oxford or Cambridge University. Wollstonecraft was raised in the Anglican faith, but the Dissenting academies that sprang up as a result of religious suppression contributed to her philosophical development. The Newington Green community, which she chanced upon in the formative late 1780s, introduced her to a life of vigorous enquiry. With these influences, plus having been the child of economically unstable parents, Mary Wollstonecraft deliberately set out on the path of personal and political improvement and independence that resulted in an exceptional contribution to human history. Most important, she incorporated feminist analysis into bourgeois liberal thought. The philosophical core of this approach drew from the argument of natural rights, which states, as Catherine Macaulay says in *Letters on Education*, that "there is but one rule of right for the conduct of all rational beings."[1]

The change she sought in women's condition varied according to class and illustrates contradictions in her political perspective. From aristocratic women she expected little, for she considered them to be in an artificial state of luxury and indolence, denied any incentive to use their talents; laboring women had potential, but she thought they would have to be led by their bourgeois sisters who, of all women, were closest to a natural state. Hannah More's sharply tiered concept of women and education had more in common with Wollstonecraft's view than is generally credited, although More deplored where Wollstonecraft supported the French Revolution, a function of a conservative as opposed to a liberal political approach. That said, it must also be stressed that Wollstonecraft's philosophy was potentially although not explicitly revolutionary, because she wanted to replace the old authoritative order by a system based on individual talent and reason, in accordance with the new liberal order of which she was, both in ideology and class origin, a member.

When she expressed her will to Johnson early in her career—"I am determined . . . ! I never yet resolved to do anything of consequence, that I did not adhere resolutely to it . . ."[2]—she was preparing herself for her contribution to history and for the struggle by way of direct action and writing that constitutes her chief legacy and her greatest significance. Wollstonecraft sized up this contribution to history in *A Vindication of the Rights of Woman* with a grand but realistic sentence: "I speak of the improvement and emancipation of the whole sex."[3] But how did a mostly self-taught woman from the petty bourgeois class put her experiences to the service of improving people's circumstances through her writings and actions?

Eighteenth-century women's lives allowed for the option of work (if their class permitted an occupation), motherhood (regardless of class), or a less orthodox choice. Wollstonecraft undertook all three. She started her career as a chaperone, then later became a teacher and afterwards a governess, three of the few jobs socially acceptable to women of her class. She then opted for the unexceptional, given her decision as an adolescent not to marry. Her experience in teaching and writing about education enabled her to "form some idea of the whole of my existence." That part of her twenties endured in disagreeable service to affluent middle-class and aristocratic employers, both demanding and indolent, tested her endurance, exposed her to social inequities, and intensified her reservations about the treatment of women. Sick relatives and friends taxed her energies and personal peace and increased these reservations. Such experiences shaped and motivated her quest for justice that resulted in public and private writings, which in turn disclosed the consequences of this life as an unconventional eighteenth-century woman.

Before the French Revolution, she punctuated her formally derivative, awkwardly executed works with personal insights. Their soul-searching honesty and frequent self-righteousness betrayed early signs of the didactic style she worked to perfect until her untimely death.

Parts of these early works read like rehearsals for the *Vindications*, the inchoate polemics of a hesitant, inexperienced, moralistic, or sentimental writer. The *Vindications* themselves are full-scale treatments, bolder, more acidic, and carefully analyzed, the style sized up for effect, their mood one of anger and passion. In her final year, she lovingly instructed mothers about infant care, and children about learning to read; she reserved political debate for her fiction, deeming it the form best calculated to reach a wide popular audience.

Luck featured prominently in her life. She was lucky to settle amid the Dissenters in Newington Green, lucky to sample an aristocratic life and hence sharpen her political understanding during her work with the Kingsborough family, and luckiest of all to acquire Johnson as her publisher, and through him to become deeply involved in radical intellectual circles in Britain and the continent. Her vision and talent, however, were never a question of luck.

Ideas

A spirit that refused acquiescence to the will of others or the circumstances of her epoch, her wide reading, and the growing circle of friends from the intelligentsia influenced her gradually but acutely. Publicly, she responded to these influences with didactic writings. She also tended in her personal life to act upon what she learned. Although she could neither have known of nor read every work by pioneer feminists, she was certainly familiar with the general tenor of their ideas in the context of eighteenth-century philosophical thought. Earlier tracts on the necessity for female education, the actions and ideas of Mary Astell, Lady Mary Wortley Montagu, the unknown Sophia, Sarah Scott, Catherine Macaulay, the Bluestockings, and revolutionary sympathizers such as Helen Maria Williams, directly and indirectly contributed to her development.

The North American and French revolutions, coupled with the historical transition from an agricultural to an industry-based economy at home, inevitably energized her thinking. These events also helped her to reformulate and synthesize what had been rather unsystematically evolving intellectual growth during years of private observation. *Thoughts on the Education of Daughters, Original Stories, Mary, A Fiction, The Female Reader,* and other prerevolutionary works were her first attempts to articulate how she analyzed and experienced her

world. Similarly, her two *Vindications* and all her later works, whatever their formal variety, continued to be instructional in spirit, since
Wollstonecraft always cherished education as a basic principle and
a necessary means of improving and transforming the social order.

Her original view of education as a vehicle to develop women's
rights locates her solidly in the radical tradition in which education
functions as a key component of social change. Shorn of indoctrination
and rote learning, education would promote the human capacity to
reason and hence to self- and social betterment. On this point she
concurred with Joseph Priestley and Thomas Day, whose *History of
Sandford and Merton* she reviewed and admired.[4] In the nineteenth
century, Jeremy Bentham, James Mill, and Robert Owen sought to
implement those ideas in different ways.[5] Owen, for example, in the
third essay of his *New View of Society* (1814), echoed the ideas of
educational reformers such as Wollstonecraft when he asserted that
the child must be "trained to be rational." Both agreed that since
education shapes any society for good or ill, a good educational system repays a lifetime fight. In this early phase, she also believed that
education, intellectual advancement, and virtue were inextricably and
continuously interrelated: women had to be rational to be virtuous. As
her political analysis sharpened, however, she began to judge education as one part of that process (rather than the process itself) that
would secure full equality for women. From her earlier notion that
education should be essentially moral in content and prepare the
soul for the afterlife, she moved to the idea that education must
prepare and refine the mind, with struggle in this world its ultimate
goal. In the end, as she instructed her daughter in the powers of
rational thinking, she concluded that moral training could and would
probably take care of itself.

Wollstonecraft varied in her religious beliefs. As far back as she
could remember, according to William Godwin in his memoirs, she
reacted contemptuously to the doctrines of innate depravity and pre-
destination and the notion of a vengeful God, although she held to
the idea of evil as part of the divine plan as late as *The Rights of Men.*
She suspected public piety, distrusted charities (finally), scorned forced
religion in public schools, shunned Sunday observance, and abhorred
both Roman Catholicism with its trappings and the "fanatical spirit"
of Methodism. All her life she was sympathetic to forms of ritual
that conduced to a spiritual frame of mind, although she disliked

them when they degenerated into theatrical show as in France during the Revolution. She hated the association between the Church of England and the state. Setting Richard Price, the Dissenting minister, "high on the scale of moral excellence" in *The Rights of Men*, she described her admiration for his preaching, "praying with all the simple energy of unaffected piety ... inculcating the dignity of virtue."[6]

In *The Rights of Woman* Wollstonecraft continued to express her belief in a being "whose judgment never swerves from the eternal rule of right" and in the power that human beings can derive from spiritual contemplation: "The humble mind that seeketh to find favour in His sight, and calmly examines its conduct when only His presence is felt will seldom form a very erroneous opinion of its own virtues."[7] By 1796, however, when she wrote *Letters from Sweden*, she displayed considerable anger over the kind of piety that becomes an unthinking system by which people are to live. As reason cut a swathe through her traditional religious beliefs, she embraced a faith essentially humanitarian in spirit, connected with no formal framework. Perhaps influenced by his own beliefs, William Godwin dismissed an apparently religious deathbed statement, while elsewhere in his memoirs he stated, "Mary had been bred in the principles of the church of England," but "her religion was, in reality, little allied to any system of forms; and, as she often told me, was founded rather in taste, than in the niceties of polemical discussion. . . . When she walked amidst the wonders of nature, she was accustomed to converse with her God . . . and her religion was almost entirely of her own creation."[8] Godwin claimed that her discontinuance of church attendance after 1787 did not preclude her belief in eternal life. She also retained a loving apprehension of the "animating spirit" that pervades nature, itself a source of meditation and reverence.[9] Despite the elevation of this belief to a moral principle by the early nineteenth century, Wollstonecraft went to her grave branded a heretic.

She also rejected arbitrary authority such as held by the army and the church, especially in the two *Vindications*; she deplored money-grubbing (particularly after she met Imlay), and assessed the early effects of competition and avarice as injurious to humanity's health. She came to view wealth and rank as fundamental sources of psychological oppression and economic exploitation. In her political transitional period, Wollstonecraft scarcely had an inkling of the labor-owner antagonism of nineteenth- and twentieth-century society. But in *The French Revolution* she did note the deadening effects of the assembly line and the clash of interest between the owner wishing to make money and the worker wishing to enjoy the work. Nonetheless, inchoate vignettes of men in the military, of Jemima with her overlord, of the frustrated lives of night watchmen in *The Wrongs of Women*, and of herself as an economically dependent chaperone and teacher, very faintly contradict her predominant view that members of the middle class are and will be the liberators of humanity.

In her opposition to the old feudal aristocratic order and its attitudes toward the treatment of women, Wollstonecraft agreed with Locke and Rousseau not only that individuals should exercise their talents and have an equal opportunity to do so, but that women must be included. Motherhood as a vocation should also be treated with respect, and in a sense Wollstonecraft equated this "occupation" with occupations in law and medicine to which she sought access for women.

The explicitly feminist ideas that she advanced partially echoed those of such earlier analysts as Mary Astell, who argued that knowledge and education brought virtuous conduct in their wake, and that the education of mothers meant a more educated, aware, virtuous citizenry.[10] Wollstonecraft concurred that the same home-bound but educated mother must be everywhere, but women must also have the option to be lawyers and doctors if they wished. She never explained how or if these phenomena would occur simultaneously. Presumably, women who wanted to work would do so, and their participation and contribution would necessarily improve the level of civilized society. She had sympathy for the endless toil of the poor, but she eschewed concrete proposals for the amelioration of their condition.

Wollstonecraft also saw marriage as an unpredictable situation for women, and even in her own case she gambled her judgment and instinct in her marriage to Godwin. In private letters, in both works of fiction, and elsewhere, if she did not speak disparagingly of marriage she at least recommended extreme caution and offered innumerable examples of the problems the institution brings to women's lives, rich, poor, and middling alike.

Before Wollstonecraft, none had contributed so significantly to women's literature and feminist thought. What made her output particularly important (and poignant) was the fact that she never shirked from trying hard, often unsuccessfully, to match her public, private, and professional lives, to do what she thought best, law or no law, convention or no convention. She tried to help her sister leave her husband, despite the inevitable cost; she wrote fictionally about her love for Fanny Blood after her death; she defended Price, although her publisher had to encourage her work's completion; she ventured and failed to arrange a highly unconventional relationship with Henry and Sophie Fuseli; she went alone to Paris during the Revolution in an action that would be viewed as intrepid in any comparable revolutionary era; she wrote a partially antagonistic book on France while remaining in that country; she bore a child out of wedlock from choice and raised it as a single parent; she ended up conceiving another child out of wedlock, and in marrying to obtain some social peace she had to expose that she had not formerly been married.

Finally, she did achieve emotional rest in her life. Done with Imlay, done with the subterfuge of her fake union with him, she married an intellectual equal and an individual who respected and loved her. For this reason her view of women in her last writings probably was more detached and more sympathetic than it had been in her earlier works. Her shift in political analysis and in her approach to women is obvious from a comparison of the titles of her two novels. In 1788 the title *Mary, A Fiction* focused on the character and, not very subtly, pointed up the author's semiautobiography. Nine years later in *The Wrongs of Woman, or Maria*, she placed the focus on what had concerned her since she came to political consciousness, the wrongs done to women. To ensure that the general could be extrapolated from the specific and individual, she added *Maria*. That she used her own name or a version of it in both also suggests the I don't-care attitude of a woman who had nothing to lose or scorned to hide her life experiences from the world.

Her final perspective on education can also be gleaned from *Hints* (1797) in which she opened with an attack on indolence; stressed that female vanity, self-absorption, and corrupt pastimes stem from the lack of a steady educational diet; and reiterated that virtue is founded on reason and that some individuals, disparagingly referred to as "the mob," need the staff of Christianity.[11] Since people cannot be virtuous without using reason, she argued, it is no wonder that uneducated middle-class women end up acting injudiciously and thoughtlessly, without due care for their children.

Mary Wollstonecraft held abolitionist views on the question of slavery, but she never wrote a systematic attack on its abuses. Both her social circles, earlier at Newington Green and later around Joseph Johnson, opposed slavery in principle.[12] In *The Female Reader* (1789) she introduced writings from William Cowper entitled "On Slavery" and "The Bastille," and in her translation of *Elements of Morality* (1790) she altered a story so that a soldier who is frightened by devils (too frightening for children) becomes frightened by Indians, yet ends up being rescued by an Indian. Elsewhere, when she called *women* slaves, she made her contempt for all slave-master relationships very plain. In *Letters from Sweden* she also talked about the oppressive conditions of the workers and peasants under tyrannical regimes, and in *The French Revolution* she described the long endurance of the French under the yoke of corrupt feudal rule.

Development of Style

Mary Wollstonecraft's style flowed directly from her experiences and ideas. With the exception of her unfinished writings, she tended to write reactively in short order or on impulse. When she sought money for the Blood family, she wrote *Thoughts on the Education of Daughters*, a brief work with no certain principle of organization beyond the casual theme of what she knew about: young women's education. The preface to *The Female Reader* addressed the same theme with a planned but rather awkward attempt to introduce principles of organization. She wrote *Original Stories* after her stint as a governess when she so disapproved of Lady Kingsborough's treatment of her children. Hence *Original Stories* diverges from *Thoughts* in being more explicitly a moral manual to guide children to rectitude, its tone conventionally stern and unyielding, the same tone with which Wollstonecraft admonished her sisters in her correspondence, if they failed to write.

Undoubtedly, her work for the *Analytical Review* aided her progress as a writer, forcing her to apply her ideas while she was improving her skills. Her constant critiques in the *Review* also served her well when she decided to respond to Burke. In fact the discursive style of the pamphlet outfitted as moral essay suited her much more temperamentally and intellectually than the previous self-contained, schematized, derivative manuals for children and adults. In the two

Vindications she could plunge head-first into her material and create striking embellishments within lengthy syntactical structures, laced with hyperbole and high-pitched emotion. She sustained this pitch until she was out of breath, done with the argument. Her earnest passion and conviction propelled the prose; the force of her intellect supplied staying power. Adapting Hartley's psychological theories of association to her literary style, she went from point to point as if in a race against herself to tell all and tell it quickly, only pausing for seeming digressions which in reality reinforced her argument.

Like Jemima, in her personal history Wollstonecraft renounced mystification, although she was not beyond the purple passage. She presented argument with extensive evidence, vivifying it with images and analogues, her form flowing naturally from the ferocious gravity of her controlling ideas. But the fluency of her prose and her supple agility in covering a wide area of ideas also permitted her to enhance her argument as she was bent on a conclusion. Her long years (one suspects) of involved conversations and complex letter writing plus what she had learned, heard, and read in more formal contexts produced this inimitable style.

In her writing decade Wollstonecraft progressed from a discursive, derivative, sometimes tight-lipped form that encased her ideas rather haphazardly, to the more systematically organized style of the two *Vindications*. This complemented her ideas better, but still kept the argument expansive and associative rather than concise and rigorous. Use of repetition, intentional or not, marked all this writing. *The French Revolution* forced her to subordinate associations to chronology and theme. In the end she had to wrestle with her style mightily because its growing structure fought her temperament. That is one of the reasons why *The Wrongs of Woman* took her so long and why many of its paragraphs are even more dense and arguably richer (given that it is fiction) than the earlier, more acclaimed political writings. Probably in *The Wrongs of Woman* she was serving another kind of apprenticeship, becoming more conscious and painstaking with her plot and organization. She rewrote and reorganized continually to develop skills that the speed and complexity of her former life and writings had not permitted her, although *The French Revolution* and *Letters from Sweden* provided her insight into an experience with a more tempered, cautious art. Hence also the many tentative conclusions to *The Wrongs of Woman*. Neither *Mary, A*

Fiction nor the polemics has the same feeling of countless drafts about them. They sound more pell-mell. Everything before 1797 (except possibly *The French Revolution*) reads as if it could have been, in tone if not in form and sometimes in both, a gigantic, complicated, sprawling letter from an animated, brilliant, and often visionary natural intelligence.

Yet Wollstonecraft was not uneducated. Her schooling in Yorkshire was assuredly competent and she certainly made up later in intellectual companionship what she had lacked in formal learning. That aside, except for Johnson's editing, she remained largely untutored until her last years, when Godwin urged her to more formal instruction. The erractic education tells in her style. She set out to rectify this in *The Wrongs of Woman* or, perhaps more accurately, she was charting a new writing course when she died. Her potential for success consequently can never be judged. Dialogue, dramatic effect, and natural description did not come easily to her, although she worked hard at them. Whether or not she required a new style to suit a philosophy that embraced increasingly more sophisticated discriminations might be yet another question.

Scope, Progress, and Influence of Wollstonecraft's Writings

By the end of her life the time for many, but not all, of Wollstonecraft's ideas had come. In *The Rights of Woman* she called for women's suffrage, the first conscious, public articulation by a woman of a demand that would receive more attention a hundred years later, but would not legally be enacted until the twentieth century. Still debated and ridiculed is an issue at which she hinted for a coequal (but class-biased) parliament, expressed in the following passage.

I cannot help lamenting that women of a superior cast have not a road open by which they can pursue more extensive plans of usefulness and independence. I may excite laughter by dropping a hint which I mean to pursue some future time, for I really think that women ought to have representatives, instead of being arbitrarily governed without having any direct share allowed them in the deliberations of government.

But as the whole system of representation is now in this country only a convenient handle for despotism, they need not complain, for they are as well represented as a numerous class of hard-working mechanics, who pay for the support of royalty when they can hardly stop their children's mouths with bread.[13]

⚡Her words on women's education and learned vanity also ring true today as they did in eighteenth-century England: "Taught from their infancy that beauty is woman's sceptre, the mind shapes itself to the body, and, roaming round its gilt cage, only seeks to adorn its prison."[14] ⚡ For many years Wollstonecraft argued that education would transform females into rational beings with middle-class women as "natural" leaders. Women "of a superior cast" should be physicians, midwives, owners and managers of small business; they should become, in a word, economically independent. By the year of her death she was promoting similar ideas in her novel fragment, but with a deeper comprehension based on accumulated experience. In *The Wrongs of Woman* she exposed a legal system that refused to right wrongs. She pointed to other systems and institutions such as hospitals, asylums, the family in some cases, and military service that conspired in the plot against laboring and middle-class people who, she was well aware, comprised an overwhelming majority of the population.

Whereas until 1791 she considered education among her major concerns, by 1791 she saw it as an inadequate tool for women's advancement. In *The Rights of Woman* education is a preparation for the afterlife; in *The Wrongs of Woman* education helps, but she had become more conscious that this world contains great problems. By the time she wrote *The Rights of Woman*, she no longer treated as ends in themselves the acquisition of virtue and knowledge through the exercise of reason and the regulation of passion. She had become persuaded that reason alone could not ameliorate social and political evils, for people like the powerful judge in *The Wrongs of Woman* will act reasonably only in self-interest. To sustain and deepen this analysis Wollstonecraft would probably have had to embrace a richer theoretical framework and a more international outlook.

Her perspective on class differences contained some contradictions. She blamed the aristocracy for inequalities of rank and saw the middle class as liberators of humanity, a common view in this epoch when the bourgeois were the revolutionaries. Thus she saw no class antagonism in the bourgeois keeping servants provided they were treated humanely. Yet she maintained strongly her desire for an end to the tyranny of rich over poor.

Mary Wollstonecraft was a remarkable woman and a remarkable writer who analyzed and proposed solutions to women's psychological and economic oppression and political exploitation. Those seventeenth-century well-to-do women—the Duchess of Newcastle was one—who wrote about women's denied rights enjoyed the leisure to contemplate such matters. Similarly, their eighteenth-century counterparts such as Wollstonecraft's own favorite, Catherine Macaulay, were not motivated by economic need. Yet such impecunious writers as Mary Pix, Catherine Trotter, Mary Delarivière Manley, Mary Davys, and Sarah Fielding defended, both indignantly and quietly, the right of women to earn a living. These twin factors, financial need and political commitment, motivated Wollstonecraft.

Moreover, as a bourgeois intellectual in a revolutionary epoch, she surpassed the thinking of earlier feminists such as Mary Astell who tended to concentrate on certain issues of concern to women. Wollstonecraft probed for a larger synthesis that would take into account a much wider range of oppression. She raised all the questions she could think of at once. If her early works represented the times with the occasional injection of acceptable forward-looking ideas, from 1792 onward she was unacceptable, dishonored as a prophet, because it was not, as she boasted, "according to my nature to mince matters."[15] Finding the cause of feminism in need of drastic attention and courageous enough to withstand conservative wrath, she characteristically seized the opportunity to make a permanent contribution to the history of human thought. In a century of innovative political ideas and fundamental historical change, she flamboyantly urged her feminist theories on the public. Although scarcely the first such theorist (and she did not claim to be), she attracted more opposition and mockery than any of her predecessors, for she was not aristocratic, wealthy, well educated, pious, or ladylike. In popular parlance, especially had her true relationship with Imlay been known, she would have been dubbed "fallen." Instead, in her hard-working, intellectually acute, and belligerent style, overlaid with her sense of moral justice, she displayed the same characteristics as the seventeenth-century bourgeois revolutionaries in whose footsteps she trod.

Any contemporary anthology of women's history, philosophy, politics, or sociology invariably includes either a tribute to Wollstonecraft or a contribution from her; sometimes she receives a mention in the dedication. Sociologist Alice Rossi found Wollstonecraft a crucial pioneer when she asserted that "Women and men in the 1970s who enjoy a wider range of sexual and social opinions are indebted for their greater latitude and freedom to such pioneers as Wollstonecraft."[16] Nearly a century earlier, in 1889 when Susan B. Anthony and Elizabeth Cady Stanton published their first three volumes of *The History of Woman Suffrage*, Mary Wollstonecraft headed the list of early feminists to whom their work was dedicated. Historian Eleanor Flexner in *Century of Struggle*, a history of the women's movement in the United States, pronounced that "the modern woman's rights movement is usually dated" from the time of Wollstonecraft's second *Vindication*.[17] According to philosopher Simone de Beauvoir in *The Second Sex*, Wollstonecraft "sketched out" the (women's rights movement in England.[18] Most recently, socialist-feminist critic Zillah Eisenstein in *The Radical Future of Liberal Feminism* acknowledged Wollstonecraft's tremendous influence.[19]

In the second century after Wollstonecraft's death, Virginia Woolf proclaimed her past and present contribution to history. Blunt and passionate, across the centuries, one abused feminist called to another:

She died in child-birth. She whose sense of her own existence was so intense, who had cried out even in her misery, "I cannot bear to think of being no more—of losing myself—nay, it appears to me impossible that I should cease to exist," died at the age of thirty-six. But she has her revenge. Many millions have died and been forgotten in the hundred and thirty years that have passed since she was buried; and yet as we read her letters and listen to her arguments and consider her experiments, above all that most fruitful experiment, her relation with Godwin, and realise the high-handed and hot-blooded manner in which she cut her way to the quick of life, one form of immortality is hers undoubtedly: she is alive and active, she argues and experiments, we hear her voice and trace her influence even now among the living.[20]

More than for most authors, Mary Wollstonecraft's works reflected her difficult and complex confrontation with life. A psychologically grim childhood and adolescence finely tuned her sensitivity to people and things. In the same way, early exposure to poverty in England and Portugal and to affluence within her middle-class and aristocratic employers' households apprised her of what she later came to see as indefensible class divisions within society. Later, in part by good fortune, she associated with people like Richard Price, whose concern it was to analyze and ameliorate inequities and to live humanely themselves. Within the circle of her publisher and his friends she became part of the radical intelligentsia. From there, she went on to inspect the French Revolution at first hand and found it ultimately worthy of admiration.

She welded the connection between the ideals of social revolution and her original intuitive awareness of women's need to rise from their degraded status, a connection that remains firm down to our own times. In articles, reviews, children's books, educational tracts, histories, polemics, textbooks, and novels, Wollstonecraft proclaimed the new feminist viewpoint. In her works may be found a chronicle of an epoch; in her life may be found a personal embodiment of those same tumultuous times.

Notes and References

Chapter One

1. For details of the inheritance see Eleanor Flexner, *Mary Wollstonecraft: A Biography* (New York: 1972), Appendix A, pp. 267–68.
2. For a full discussion of gentleman farming, see E. J. Hobsbawm, *Industry and Empire* (New York: Pantheon Books, 1968), 1st Am. ed.; Chapter 5. In Chapter 1 of *A Different Face: The Life of Mary Wollstonecraft* (New York: Harper & Row, 1975), p. 11, Emily Sunstein persuasively speculates that Henry Wollstonecraft, of whom there is next to no mention, might have been mentally unstable. This would explain Wollstonecraft's sympathy for and interest in madness and asylums.
3. William Godwin, *Memoirs and Posthumous Works of Mary Wollstonecraft Godwin, Author of a Vindication of the Rights of Woman*, 2 vols. (Dublin: Thomas Burnside, 1798) 1:6. Subsequently this edition is referred to as *Memoirs* or *Posthumous Works*. (Godwin's *Memoirs* end on page 117 of the first volume and the *Posthumous Works* follow.) *Posthumous Works* is hereafter cited in the title as *PW*.
4. Virginia Woolf, *The Second Common Reader* (New York: Harcourt, Brace & Co., 1932), p. 142.
5. The money settled on the Wollstonecraft children (except for Edward [Ned] who, as the eldest, received one-third of his grandfather's fortune) is something of a mystery. See Godwin, *Memoirs*, 1:25. See also Mary Wollstonecraft's letter to Jane Arden in *Shelley and His Circle* (Cambridge: Harvard University Press, 1961, 1970), Kenneth N. Cameron, editors, 2:96; and Appendix A in Flexner, *Mary Wollstonecraft*, (New York, 1972), pp. 267–68. The provisions of her grandfather's will made Wollstonecraft suffer from and resent the practice of primogeniture all her life. See Tomalin (London, 1974), pp. 4–5 for the will and Flexner (New York, 1972), pp. 63, 74, and elsewhere for her poor relationship with her eldest brother, Edward.
6. The facts of Wollstonecraft's life included here come from her own writings, especially her letters and novels, from Godwin's *Memoirs*; from later biographies by Elizabeth Robins Pennell, *Mary Wollstonecraft Godwin* (London: W. H. Allen & Co., 1893); George R. Stirling Taylor, *Mary Wollstonecraft: A Study in Economics and Romance* (New York: Haskell House, 1969); Wardle, *Mary Wollstonecraft* (Lawrence: Uni-

versity of Kansas Press, 1951); Eleanor Flexner, *Mary Wollstonecraft* (New York, 1972), Claire Tomalin, *The Life and Death of Mary Wollstonecraft* (London, 1974); Emily Sunstein, *A Different Face* (New York, 1975); and the first four volumes of *Shelley and His Circle*, K. N. Cameron, ed.

7. Godwin, *Memoirs*, 1:13.

8. See the recent work by Lillian Faderman, *Surpassing the Love of Men: Romantic Friendship and Love Between Women from the Renaissance to the Present* (New York, 1981), which carefully illustrates this phenomenon among women. For a discussion of Anna Howe and Clarissa, see Chapter 1 of Janet Todd, *Women's Friendship in Literature* (New York, 1980).

9. Ralph Wardle, ed., *Collected Letters* (Ithaca and London, 1979), p. 105.

10. Mary Wollstonecraft, *Letters Written During a Short Residence in Sweden, Norway, and Denmark*, ed. Carol H. Poston (Lincoln, 1976), p. 59. Subsequent references are to this edition, with its shortened title, *Letters from Sweden*.

11. Flexner, *Mary Wollstonecraft*, p. 289, note 10.

12. Mary Wollstonecraft, *Thoughts on the Education of Daughters* (London, 1787), pp. 69–78. Subsequent references are to this edition.

13. Godwin, *Memoirs*, 1:16–17. Wollstonecraft's attitude to primogeniture is discussed more fully in Chapter 4, p. 52, in this volume.

14. Fanny Blood to Everina Wollstonecraft, February 1782 (reel IX), from the Lord Abinger Collection. These letters were made available through the courtesy of the Carl H. Pforzheimer Library, New York.

15. Some discrepancies exist regarding the dates of Eliza's marriage, confinement, and escape. Eleanor Flexner sets the date of Eliza's marriage as October 10, 1782, and the birth of Eliza's daughter "a few weeks later," with information from documents found in the London Guildhall by Eleanor Nicholes. That Mr. Wollstonecraft's consent was sworn near Laugharne on October 4, 1782, causes Flexner to conclude that Eliza was pregnant at the time of marriage. Tomalin dates the marriage October 20, 1782, but dates the birth of the daughter August 10, 1783, citing the christening record at Bermondsey parish church. Sunstein also argues for October 20, and agrees on August 10, 1783.

16. Wardle, ed., *Collected Letters*, p. 86.

17. Women could not have legal custody of their children in any circumstances. For accounts of the legal status of women see Leo Kanowitz, *Women and the Law* (Albuquerque: University of New Mexico Press, 1969), especially Chapters 1 and 2; L. P. Brockert, *Woman: Her Rights, Wrongs, Privileges, and Responsibilities* (1869; reprint ed., Freeport,

N.Y.: Books for Libraries Press, 1970), Chapter 4; and William Blackstone, *Commentaries on the Laws of England*, 2d ed. (Chicago: Callaghan & Co., 1879) especially the chapter entitled "Of Husband and Wife."

18. Ralph M. Wardle, ed., *Godwin and Mary: Letters of William Godwin and Mary Wollstonecraft* (Lincoln and London: University of Nebraska Press, 1977), p. 28.

19. Wardle, ed., *Collected Letters*, p. 108.

20. For a discussion of Lord Kingsborough as an improving agriculturist, see Tomalin, *Life and Death*.

21. Wardle, ed., *Collected Letters*, p. 140.

22. Ibid., p. 167. This again emphasizes the strong emotional relationships that Mary Wollstonecraft had with several women. Claire Tomalin suggests in *Life and Death*, p. 18 and note that she was bisexual. Carrol Smith-Rosenberg, in a different historical context, in an article entitled "The Female World of Love and Ritual: Relations between Women in Nineteenth Century America," *Signs* 1, no. 1 (1975): 1–29, concludes that similar relationships were probably not sexual in most instances.

23. Margaret Kingsborough, who at nineteen married the Earl of Mountcashel, became an Irish republican and atheist and defended Mary Wollstonecraft throughout her life. In 1803 she left her husband, settled in Italy (calling herself Mrs. Mason after Wollstonecraft's fictional character in *Original Stories*), and became acquainted with Mary and Percy Bysshe Shelley. Her relationship with Wollstonecraft is discussed in Edward C. McAleer, *The Sensitive Plant* (Chapel Hill, 1950).

24. Wardle, ed., *Collected Letters*, p. 164.

25. Mary Wollstonecraft held the position of reviewer for the monthly *Analytical Review* from its inception in May 1788 until late 1792, when she left for Paris to see for herself the effects of the French Revolution. She began again about the middle of 1796, when she had discontinued her relationship with Gilbert Imlay and was back in London; she continued until about May 1797, shortly before her death.

26. For a discussion of Wollstonecraft's contributions to the *Analytical Review* see Wardle, "Mary Wollstonecraft, Analytical Reviewer," *PMLA* 62 (December 1947): 1000–1009; and Flexner, *Mary Wollstonecraft*, pp. 273–74.

27. Selections from the reviews of novels and educational works are reprinted in *A Wollstonecraft Anthology*, ed. Janet Todd (Bloomington, 1977).

28. Wollstonecraft translated Jacques Necker's *De l'importance des opinions religieuses* and J. H. Campe's *New Robinson Crusoe* (probably from the French translation of the German) at the end of 1788. In 1789 she began to revise (from the Dutch) Madame de Cambon's *Young*

Grandison and translated Johann Kaspar Lavater's *Physiognomie* from the German. Later in 1790 she translated Christian Gotthilf Salzmann's *Moralisches Elementärbuch* (*Elements of Morality*).

29. The anthology for women that she compiled, *The Female Reader*, was considered lost until very recently, when editions were discovered at Duke University, the British Library, and Vassar College.

30. Mary Wollstonecraft, *An Historical and Moral View of the Origin and Progress of the French Revolution, and the Effect It has produced in Europe* (London, 1794; New York: Scholars Facsimiles and Reprints, 1975), 1:17. As an example of her earlier religious views, consider the spring of 1788 when she asked John Hewlett to write a sermon about meeting loved ones in paradise, an obvious reference to her belief that she would meet Fanny Blood again.

31. *Analytical Review*, 5 (October 1789):218.

32. *Analytical Review*, 8 (November 1790):246.

33. Godwin states that Ann was "the niece of Mrs. John Hunter, and, the present Mrs. Skeys, for whose mother, then lately dead, she had entertained a sincere friendship" (*Memoirs*, p. 49); Claire Tomalin calls her Hugh Skeys's cousin, while Flexner, *Mary Wollstonecraft*, p. 29, note 3, states that "according to the *Journal* of Ezra Stiles (then president of Yale University), Ann was an orphan whom the dying mother, an East Indian, asked Mary to bring up." The practice of fostering out children to childless people was common at the time; the reason for Ann's dismissal is unclear.

34. Mrs. Paget Toynbee, ed., *The Letters of Horace Walpole* (Oxford: Oxford University Press, 1905), 15:121–32, 337–38.

35. Wardle, ed., *Collected Letters*, p. 218.

36. Wollstonecraft, *Letters from Sweden*, pp. 85, 127.

37. Wardle, ed., *Godwin and Mary*, p. 17.

Chapter Two

1. For a good account of the development of sex roles, see Ruth Bloch, "Untangling the Roots of Modern Sex Roles: A Survey of Four Centuries of Change," *Signs* (Winter 1978):237–53.

2. The idea that a wife's identity is contained in her husband's, that a woman is a *femme couverte*, finds popular expression in William Blackstone's *Commentaries on the Laws of England*. Mary Beard in *Women as Force in History* (London and New York: Macmillan, 1946) discusses his doctrine at some length in Chapter 4, "The Haunting Idea: Its Nature & Origin." The legal situation prior to Wollstonecraft is described carefully in Janelle Greenberg's "The Legal Status of English Women in

Early Eighteenth Century Common Law and Equity," *Studies in Eighteenth-Century Culture* 4 (1975):171–81.

3. Several courtesy books at the time recommended nothing more than cultivation of social graces and light accomplishments for young women. Among the most notable was George Savile, first Marquis of Halifax, *The Lady's New-years Gift; or Advice to a Daughter* (London: Randal Taylor, 1688), a popular manual of the late seventeenth century that outlined the kind of meek, well-mannered behavior expected of pious young women who intended to marry well (reprint by Hester Saintsbury [Kensington; Printed by P. Saintsbury, 1927]); Dr. James Fordyce, *Sermons to Young Women* (London: Printed for A. Miller and T. Cadell, 1765); and Dr. John Gregory, *A Father's Legacy to His Daughters* (London: Printed for W. Strahan, T. Cadell, W. Creech, 1774; reprint ed., New York: Garland Publishing, 1976). On the other hand, since the late seventeenth century in Britain, tracts had been published by advocates of female education: among the most celebrated were Bathsua Makin, (influenced by the notable continental scholar Anna von Schurman), *An Essay to revive the antient Education of Gentlewomen, in religion, manners, arts and tongues with an Answer to the Objectives against this Way of Education* (London: J. D. for Thomas Parkhurst, 1673); Mary Astell, *A Serious Proposal to the Ladies for the Advancement of Their Time and Greatest Interest, in Two Parts.* (London, 1694, 1697; reprint ed., New York: Source Book Press, 1970); and Daniel Defoe, *An Essay on Projects* (London, 1698); reprinted in *Eighteenth Century Poetry and Prose*, ed. Louis Bredvold, Alan McKillop, Lois Whitney (New York: Ronald Press, 1939). A recent useful and important book on women scholars that includes an informative essay on Bathsua Makin is J. R. Brink, ed., *Female Scholars: A Tradition of Learned Women Before 1800* (Montreal: Eden Press Women's Publications, 1980). In midcentury Sarah Fielding in *The Governess; or the Little Female Academy* (London, 1749 reprinted, London: Oxford University Press, 1968) was directly and indirectly suggesting through fiction that females deserve some kind of education. Among useful works that narrate the course of female education from their earliest beginnings are Myra Reynolds, *The Learned Lady in England, 1650–1760* (Boston, New York: Houghton-Mifflin, 1920); Dorothy Gardiner, *English Girlhood at School: A Study of Women's Education Through Twelve Centuries* (London: Oxford University Press, 1929); Doris Mary Stenton, *The English Woman in History* (London: Routledge & Kegan Paul, 1957); Ida Beatrice O'Malley, *Women in Subjection: A Study of the Lives of English-women before 1832* (London: Duckworth, 1933); Josephine Kamm, *Hope Deferred: Girls' Education in English History* (London: Methuen & Co., 1965); Walter Lyon Blease, *The*

Emancipation of English Women (London: 1910); and Barbara Brandon Schnorrenberg, "Education for Women in Eighteenth Century England: An Annotated Bibliography," *Women and Literature* 4 no. 1 (Spring 1976): 49–55.

4. These schools are discussed briefly in Reynolds, *Learned Lady*, pp. 42–54. See also Philip Webster Souers, *The Matchless Orinda* (Cambridge: Harvard University Press, 1931), p. 20; Gardiner, *English Girlhood* p. 211; and Phyllis Stock, *Better Than Rubies: A History of Women's Education* (New York: G. P. Putnam's Sons, 1978), especially Chapters 3 and 4, "The Lady in Salon and Convent and School," and "The Enlightenment Debate on Women," pp. 81–125.

5. There are varied accounts of the Bluestockings, including the following: R. Huchon, *Mrs. Montagu and Her Friends* (Mrs. Montagu, 1730–1800) (London: J. Murray, 1907); R. Brimley Johnson, *Bluestocking Letters* (London: John Lane, 1926); and Marilyn L. Williamson "Who's Afraid of Mrs. Barbauld? The Bluestockings and Feminism," *International Journal of Women's Studies* 3, no. 1 (1980):89–102.

6. Two of the few books that address women as workers in early periods are Alice Clark, *Working Life of Women in the Seventeenth Century* (London: reprint ed., 1919; New York: A. M. Kelley, 1968); and Ivy Pinchbeck, *Women Workers and the Industrial Revolution, 1750–1850* (London, New York: F. S. Crofts & Co., 1930). Also see O'Malley, *Women in Subjection*, note 3.

7. Some sources for John Locke's ideas on education are: *The Educational Writings of John Locke*, ed. James Axtell (London: Cambridge University Press, 1968); Elizabeth Lawrence, *The Origin and Growth of Modern Education* (London and Baltimore: Penguin Books, 1970); Samuel Parker, *The History of Modern Elementary Education* (Boston and New York: Ginn & Co., 1912).

8. Mary Wollstonecraft, *The Female Reader* (London, 1789; facsimile, New York, 1980), p. v.

9. Wollstonecraft glowingly reviewed Macaulay's *Letters on Education* in the *Analytical Review* 8 (1790):241–54.

10. Jean-Jacques Rousseau stated this view of females as creatures whose life object is to please men in the fifth book of *Emile* (1762), which Wollstonecraft had not apparently read at this time, although she was familiar enough with Rousseau as a writer to mention him in a letter to her sister.

11. Wollstonecraft, *A Vindication of the Rights of Woman*, ed. Charles Hagelman (New York: W. W. Norton, 1967), p. 218.

12. Wollstonecraft, *Thoughts*, p. 99.

13. Godwin, *Posthumous Works*, 1:274.

14. Wollstonecraft, *Thoughts*, p. 16. Subsequent references are to this edition.

15. Wollstonecraft, *Original Stories from Real Life; with Conversations Calculated to Regulate the Affections and Form the Mind to Truth and Goodness* (London, 1788). Subsequent references are to this edition.

16. For an elaboration of Blake's aesthetic resistance to Wollstonecraft's ideas see Dennis Welch, "Blake's Response to Wollstonecraft's *Original Stories*," *Blake: An Illustrated Quarterly* 13, no. 1 (Summer 1979):4–15.

17. *Collected Letters*, p. 132. Mary to Everina Wollstonecraft, March 26, 1787 (reel IX), Lord Abinger Collection.

18. Godwin, *Posthumous Works* 1:274–79.

19. Ibid., p. 278.

20. Wollstonecraft, *The Female Reader* (London, 1788; reprint ed., New York: Scholar's Facsimiles and Reprints, 1980). Christian Salzmann, *Elements of Morality for the Use of Children,* trans. Mary Wollstonecraft (London, 1790; reprint ed., Baltimore: Joseph Robinson, 1811).

21. For information on the philosophical influences see the introduction to *The Female Reader*. For background on Salzmann, see Frank Graves, *Great Educators of Three Centuries: Their Work and its Influence on Modern Education* (New York: Macmillan Co., 1912; reprint ed., New York: AMS Press, 1971).

Chapter Three

1. See J. M. S. Tompkins, *The Popular Novel in England, 1770–1800* (London: Constable & Co., 1932) for the role and status of female novelists; Ruth Perry, *Women, Letters, and the Novel* (New York: AMS Press, 1980), especially Chapter 2, "The Economic Status of Women," pp. 27–64; and Joyce M. Horner, *The English Women Novelists and Their Connection with The Feminist Movement* (1699–1797), vol. 11, nos. 1, 2, 3, of *Smith College Studies in Modern Languages* (Northampton, Mass.. 1929–30).

2. Aphra Behn (1640–1689) was the first known professional woman writer in English. The preface to her play *The Dutch Lover* discussed the novelty of woman as writer. For an account of women writing, see also Alison Adburgham, *Women in Print* (London: Allan & Unwin, 1972).

3. Accounts of the rise of literacy may be found in Amy Cruse, *The Shaping of English Literature* (New York: Thomas Y. Crowell, 1927), and Q. D. Leavis, *Fiction and the Reading Public* (London: Chatto & Windus, 1932).

4. For accounts of the Bluestockings see note 6, Chapter 2.

5. For the rise of philanthropy see Betsy Rodgers, *Cloak of Charity:*

Studies in Eighteenth-Century Philanthropy (London: Methuen & Co., 1949). For a brief account of the growing occurrences of sentimentality in the novel see Chapter 3 of Tompkins, *Popular Novel*, pp. 70–115.

6. See Reynolds, *Learned Lady*, pp. 414–15.

7. Henry Brooke, *Fool of Quality* (London: Printed for W. Johnston, 1766–1769) and Henry Mackenzie, *The Man of Feeling* (London: T. Cadell, 1771).

8. Wollstonecraft, *Mary, A Fiction* (London, 1788, reprint ed., New York: Schocken Books, 1977), pp. 3–4. Subsequent references are to the 1977 edition.

9. Later examples of the treatment in "female fiction" of "the thinking powers of a young woman" are Mary Ann Hanway, *Ellinor, or The World as it Is* (London, 1798; reprint ed., New York: Garland Publishing, 1976), Mary Brunton, *Self-Control* (Edinburgh, 1811; reprint ed., New York: Garland Publishing, 1974), and Mary Hays, *Memoirs of Emma Courtney* (London, 1796; reprint ed., New York: Garland Publishing, 1974).

10. The double standard persistently applied, and "illicit" relationships abounded, but fictionally the Christian moral code was sanctified. Popular novels that illustrate this code include Joseph Cradock, *Village Memoirs* (London: T. Davies, 1765); Anonymous, *Peggy and Patty*, 4 vols. (London: Printed for J. A. Dodsley, 1784); in Hugh Kelly, *Memoirs of a Magdalen*, 2 vols. (London: Printed for W. Griffin, 1767), the middle-class heroine is somewhat exceptionally allowed to repent.

11. Wardle, ed., *Collected Letters*, p. 95.

12. Long, loving friendships between women were not uncommon in the eighteenth century and the letters of the Bluestocking Elizabeth Carter to Catherine Talbot, for example, attest to this. (For more information, see notes 8 and 20 in Chapter 1.) Other novels about female friends are Charlotte Lennox, *Euphemia* (London: Printed for T. Cadell and J. Evans, 1790) and Sarah Scott and Barbara Montagu, *Millenium Hall* (London: Printed for J. Newbery, 1762).

13. For a detailed account see Pinchbeck, *Women Workers* (London, New York, 1930).

14. Elizabeth Gould Davis, *The First Sex* (London: G. P. Putnam's Sons, 1971), p. 299.

15. Wollstonecraft, *Extract of the Cave of Fancy: A Tale.* (Begun in the year 1787, but never completed), in *Posthumous Works of the Author of a Vindication of the Rights of Woman*, 4 volumes in 2. London, 1798; Facsimile, Fairfield, N.J.: 1972. Subsequent references to *The Cave* (vol. 4 in vol. 2) are to this edition.

16. Johann Kasper Lavater, *Physiognomie*, trans. Thomas Holcroft (Es-

says on Physiognomie) (London, 1789), p. 9. Subsequent references are to this edition.

17. In *The Wrongs of Woman* Wollstonecraft still faintly suggested a relationship between character and physiognomy. One example is the description of the nurse of Venables's child "her eyes inflamed, with an indescribable look of cunning. . . ." Wollstonecraft seemed to agree with a link between environment and physiognomy in her review of December 1788 in the *Analytical Review* on "An Essay on the Causes of the Variety of Complection. . . .", pp. 431–39.

18. Supplement to Godwin's *Memoirs*, by W. Clark Durant (London, 1927), p. 150.

19. Godwin, *Memoirs*, 1:38.

Chapter Four

1. The enthusiasm of the Dissenters for the French Revolution was partly due to their peculiar understanding of it. They saw it at first as an imitation of the British Glorious Revolution of 1688, which had ratified some of their liberties. Since they still felt dissatisfied, they welcomed the French Revolution as the beginning of an improvement in political affairs, which should in time result in further improvement in Britain.

2. At the 1788 commemoration, three principles were adopted stating that civil and political authority was derived from the people, that the abuse of power justified resistance, and that the rights of private judgment, liberty of conscience, trial by jury, and freedom of the press and of elections should be inviolable. These principles formed the basis of Price's address. For an account of the proceedings of the Revolution Society, see Eleanor Nicholes's historical introduction to *A Vindication of the Rights of Men* (London, 1790; Gainesville, 1960). Page references in the text are to the facsimile edition.

3. Richard Price, *A Discourse on the Love of Our Country* (Dublin: H. Chamberlain, 1790), pp. 49–50.

4. In his opposition to the French Revolution, Burke broke with the Whig opinion that he had held and defended through the crisis of the American Revolution.

5. Wollstonecraft's commentary made Burke's ideas appear ridiculous by taking them to their extreme conclusion. Both reverence for the past and submission to authority were mocked in this way.

6. *Speeches of the Right Honourable Edmund Burke in the House of Commons and in Westminster-Hall* (London: Longman & Co., 1816), 3:409.

7. Price distinguished between speculative and moral reason. Moral

truths were perceived by an act of intelligence, not by the exercise of a special intuitive moral faculty. For a more detailed discussion of this, see Emma Rauschenbusch-Clough, *A Study of Mary Wollstonecraft and the Rights of Women* (London: Longmans, Green & Co., 1898); see also Chapter 3, note 8.

8. Edmund Burke, *Philosophical Enquiry into the Sublime and Beautiful* (London: Routledge and Paul, 1958), p. 116.

9. Wollstonecraft's language was frequently commented on by reviewers. Some were favorable, but most felt with the critic of the *Monthly Review* 5 (1791), that she overloaded her sentences with a "multiplicity of words."

10. Sunstein, *A Different Face*, pp. 36–38. Sunstein argues that a single late reference to Henry suggests his continued existence. Earlier, the family's removal to Hoxton, famous for its mental institutions, might have been dictated by Henry's condition.

11. See the *Gentleman's Magazine* 61 (January 1791):151–54 and the *Critical Review* 70 (1790):694–96, both of which mocked the femaleness of the author.

Chapter Five

1. Wollstonecraft, *The Rights of Woman*, p. 95. Subsequent references in the text are to the 1967 edition.

2. Hannah More, *Strictures on the Modern System of Female Education* (London: T. Cadell & G. W. Davies, 1799), 2:20. For another example of the Bluestocking opinion, see Hester Chapone's *Letters on the Improvement of the Mind, Addressed to a Young Lady* (1773); *The Works* (Boston: Wells and Wait, 1809).

3. Other ideas Macaulay anticipated include the contradiction of exhorting women to good nature while providing them with examples of the power over men of sexual attractiveness and cunning; and the similarity of men and women except in the area of physical strength. The latter idea was asserted by Macaulay and suggested by Wollstonecraft.

4. Olympe de Gouges, *Declaration des Droits de la Femme et de la Citoyenne* (1791), reprinted in *Women in Revolutionary Paris 1789–95*, ed. Darline Gay Levy, Harriet Branson Applewhite, and Mary Durham Johnson (Urbana: University of Illinois Press, 1979).

5. Jean Antoine, Marquis de Condorcet, *Oeuvres complètes*, ed. A. Condorcet O'Connor and M. F. Arago (Paris: Firmin Didot Frères, 1847–49).

6. For a description of this document, see Crane Brinton, *Lives of Talleyrand* (New York: Allen & Unwin, 1936).

7. The *Report* is printed in *French Liberalism and Education in the Eighteenth Century*, trans. and ed. Francois de la Fontainerie (New York: McGraw Hill, 1932). For a discussion of Wollstonecraft and Condorcet, see *Shelley and His Circle*, 4:872–76.

8. Wollstonecraft to Ruth Barlow, February 1793, *Shelley and His Circle*, 4:866.

9. According to Wollstonecraft's Advertisement, *The Rights of Woman* was intended as the first of two volumes; the legal and political situation of women was to have provided material for the second. This second volume was never written, and none of Wollstonecraft's later books provided a sequel, although the unfinished novel, *The Wrongs of Woman*, came closest to it in its concern for the legal inequality of men and women and for the particular injustices suffered by the poor.

10. Rousseau's view of women was complex and varied from work to work. Wollstonecraft was concerned only with the picture presented in *Emile*.

11. Godwin, *Posthumous Works*, 1:155.

12. Wollstonecraft required intellectual vigor in women, not only so that they might enter some of the male professions, but so that they could become better wives and mothers. Domestic virtue was, in her view, a product of intellect.

13. Godwin considered dangerous the alliance of government and education that a national education presupposed. It would, he believed, lead to the reinforcement of established prejudice.

14. Wollstonecraft to William Roscoe, October 1791, reprinted in Flexner, *Mary Wollstonecraft*, p. 275.

15. Horace Walpole to Hannah More, in Peter Cunningham, ed., *Letters of Horace Walpole* (London: Henry G. Bohn, 1861); letter to Eliza Wollstonecraft, quoted in Sunstein, *A Different Face*, p. 214.

16. *The Poetical Works of Robert Southey* (London: Longman, Brown, Green & Longmans, 1845); Mary Hays, *Letters and Essays, Moral and Miscellaneous* (London: Thomas Knott, 1793).

17. *Monthly Magazine and British Register* 4 (1797):232–33.

18. *Annual Necrology for 1797–8* (London: Phillips, 1800), pp. 422, 412.

19. *Critical Review, or Annals of Literature* (1792):359–98; (1792): 132–41.

20. *Monthly Review; or, Literary Journal* 8 (1792):198–209.

21. *Analytical Review* 12 (1792):241–49.

22. *Anti-Jacobin Review and Magazine: or, Monthly Political and Literary Censor* 1 (1798):94–102.

23. *Lady's Monthly Museum or Polite Repository of Amusement and Instruction* 3 (1799):433.

24. George Walker, *The Vagabond, A Novel* (London: G. Walker, 1799).

25. *Robert and Adela: or the Rights of Women best maintained by the Sentiments of Nature* (London: 1795).

Chapter Six

1. In the Advertisement, Wollstonecraft stated that she had written a "considerable part" of "two or three more volumes," but no evidence of them has been found.

2. *Analytical Review* 12 (January-April 1792):93, 101–4. The first review was unsigned but preceded a review initialled "M." The second was signed "T."

3. *A Wollstonecraft Anthology*, pp. 120–21. Louis XVI was not actually going to his death but to his trial. He was beheaded in January 1793.

4. *A Wollstonecraft Anthology*, pp. 122–24. Like her *French Revolution*, Wollstonecraft's "Letter on the Present Character of the French Nation" was supposed to have been the first of a series of works, but it was the only one completed. It was not published at the time and first appeared in *Posthumous Works*.

5. See Hedva Ben-Israel, *English Historians on the French Revolution* (Cambridge: at the University Press, 1968).

6. Arthur Young, *Travels in France* (London: 1792; reprint ed., New York: Doubleday, 1969), and *The Example of France, a Warning to Britain* (London: W. Richardson, 1793).

7. Helen Maria Williams, *Letters From France* (1790–95; New York: Scholars' Facsimiles & Reprints, 1975).

8. Other source books used by Wollstonecraft include the *Journal des Debats et des Decrets* of the National Assembly, from which she took many long speeches; the account of the first year of the Revolution by Rabaut Saint-Etienne, who was guillotined in 1793; memoirs and histories by Lally-Tollendal and Mirabeau, both important actors in the early struggles of the Revolution.

9. Wollstonecraft, *The French Revolution*, p. 26. Subsequent references in the text are to the facsimile edition.

10. See, for example, p. 247, where France is described as a "nation of women."

11. The period treated on *The French Revolution* did not contain the political actions of the most famous revolutionary women such as Madame

Roland and Theroigne de Mericourt, but lesser figures abounded and were ignored by Wollstonecraft. The role of revolutionary women was treated in detail by Lady Morgan in *France* (1817). Another book, written well after the Revolution and dedicated to the memory of Marie Antoinette, concentrated on the virtue of the revolutionary victims. Among contemporary chroniclers, Helen Maria Williams devoted many of her pages to glowing accounts of female bravery and fortitude. See her *Letters from France*.

12. There is less justification for the mixed metaphors that Wollstonecraft used liberally. These resulted in some bizarre effects, as when the lion of Liberty became hermaphrodite.

13. This reaction is surprising, since many English people at the time were being horrified by accounts of jacobin atrocities, told with fervor by exiled aristocrats.

14. The *Critical Review* 16 (1796):390–96, disliked Wollstonecraft's mixture of morality and history, while the *British Critic* 16 (1795):393–40, called the work a mere abridgment of the *New Annual Register*. On the other side, the *Analytical Review* 20 (1795):337–47, thought the book solid and impartial, and the *Monthly Review* 16 (1795):393–402, praised the account of the significance of the Revolution.

15. John Adams, "Comments on Mary Wollstonecraft's French Revolution," *Bulletin of the Boston Public Library*, Series 4, 5, no. 11 (January–March 1923):4–13.

16. The frequency of Shelley's reading of Wollstonecraft is suggested by Mary Shelley's journal. For a discussion of the influence of Wollstonecraft's *French Revolution* on Shelley, see Gerald McNiece, *Shelley and the Revolutionary Idea* (Cambridge: Harvard University Press, 1969).

Chapter Seven

1. Godwin, *Memoirs*, 1:75.
2. Wardle, *Mary Wollstonecraft*, p. 256.
3. Wollstonecraft, *Letters from Sweden*, p. xx.
4. Tomalin, *The Life and Death of Mary Wollstonecraft*, p. 189.
5. Godwin, *Memoirs*, 1:120–59. All subsequent references for *Letters to Imlay* are to this edition.
6. These nontraditional forms of women's literature are currently being resurrected and reexamined. Probably Wollstonecraft's works will assume their rightful place among several of these forms, including letters, fictionalized autobiography, the journal-diary, and the mystical confessional. Forthcoming studies will encompass this perspective on her work.
7. Gilbert Imlay, *A Topographical Description of the Western Ter-*

ritory of North America: Containing a Succinct Account of Its Soil, Climate, Natural History, Population, Agriculture, Manners and Customs (London: Printed for J. Debrett, 1792).

8. See Catherine Smith, "Jane Lead: Mysticism and the Woman Cloathed with the Sun," *Shakespeare's Sisters: Feminist Essays on Women Poets*, ed. Sandra Gilbert and Susan Gubar (Bloomington: University of Indiana Press, 1979).

9. For a cogent sociopolitical history of Scandinavia, see S. M. Toyne, *The Scandinavians in History* (New York: Longmans, Green & Co., 1948).

10. During the reign of Frederick IV, Denmark suffered town and country plague, a destructive west coast tidal wave, and a series of fires, including the one mentioned by Wollstonecraft in which two-thirds of Copenhagen was razed. During his reign, in conjunction with Count Bernstoff, Frederick established a comprehensive educational system that resulted in the emancipation of the (literate) peasants in 1792, an act Wollstonecraft praised. Higher education in schools and universities was also promoted.

11. For a full account of Struensee's role in Danish royal history, see Toyne, pp. 238–44.

12. A fuller discussion of the bizarre circumstances of Queen Matilda's life and possible reasons for Wollstonecraft's sympathetic concern can also be found in Hester W. Chapman, *Caroline Matilda: Queen of Denmark 1751–75* (London: Cape, 1971).

13. Wollstonecraft's disillusionment with France showed through here. See Chapter 6, pp. 128–29.

14. Wollstonecraft, *Letters from Sweden*, p. 22.

15. Godwin, *Memoirs*, 1:75.

Chapter Eight

1. Works that treat the contemporary didactic fiction include Gary Kelly, *The English Jacobin Novel 1780–1805* (Oxford: Oxford University Press, 1976), which concentrates on the works of Robert Bage, Elizabeth Inchbald, Thomas Holcroft, and William Godwin; and Allene Gregory, *The French Revolution and the English Novel* (New York: G. P. Putnam's Sons, 1915), which discusses, among others, Mary Hays, Charlotte Smith, and Mary Wollstonecraft.

2. For more information about Charlotte Smith, see Florence M. S. Hilbish, "Charlotte Smith Poet and Novelist (1769–1806)," Ph.D., dissertation, University of Pennsylvania, 1941. In *The Old Manor House* the reappropriation of Madame Roker's fortune to her husband upon

marriage is one example of the legal subordination of women. See vol. 4, Chapters 6 and 8.

3. Mary Wollstonecraft's interest in prisons and asylums has been carefully documented recently by Gary Kelly in the explanatory notes to *The Wrongs of Woman* in his edition of *Mary, and the Wrongs of Woman* (Oxford, 1976); by Sunstein in her biography of Mary Wollstonecraft (New York, 1975), pp. 36–38; and in Gerald P. Tyson, *Joseph Johnson: A Liberal Publisher* (Iowa City: University of Iowa Press, 1979), pp. 88–89.

4. Wollstonecraft, *Maria, or the Wrongs of Woman* (New York, 1975), p. 136. Subsequent references are to this edition. The more customary title, *The Wrongs of Woman, or Maria*, is used throughout.

5. Frances Brooke, *The History of Emily Montagu*, 4 vols. (London: J. Dodsley, 1769); Charlotte Lennox, *Euphemia*; Charlotte Smith, *Desmond* (London: P. Wogan, 1792), and *The Old Manor House* (London: J. Bell, 1793).

6. In that they purport to be from an aggrieved mother to her daughter, these memoirs are reminiscent of Lady Sarah Pennington, *An Unfortunate Mother's Advice to Her Absent Daughters* (London: S. Chandler, 1761). For an analysis of courtesy literature, see Joyce Hemlow "Fanny Burney and the Courtesy Books," *PMLA* 65, no. 5 (September 1950).

7. On *Woman and the Law*, see Chapter 1, note 16; and Chapter 2, note 3.

8. Wollstonecraft states: "She wrote a paper, which she expressly desired might be read in court." Perhaps Wollstonecraft would have had Maria read the statement to challenge the notion that women could not speak in court.

9. For a more detailed discussion of *The Wrongs of Woman* as a fight against sensibility, see Todd, *Women's Friendship in Literature* (New York, 1980), and Janet Todd, "Reason and Sensibility in Mary Wollstonecraft's *The Wrongs of Woman*," *Frontiers* 5, no. 3 (1980):17–20.

10. Henry Mayhew, *London Labour and the London Poor* (New York: Dover Publications, 1968), vol. 4.

11. *Collected Letters*, p. 391.

12. *Fragments of Letters on the Management of Infants*, vol. 4 in volume 2, from *Posthumous Works* edition in Chapter 3, footnote 14, pp. 55–57.

13. Wollstonecraft, *The Wrongs of Woman*, pp. 119–20.

14. Godwin, *Memoirs*, 1:100. See also Wardle, ed., *Godwin and Mary*, pp. 27–29, 35.

15. Godwin, *Memoirs*, 1:107.

Chapter Nine

1. Catherine Macaulay, *Letters on Education: with observations on religious and metaphysical subjects* (London, 1970; reprint, ed., London, New York: Garland Publishing, 1974).

2. Godwin, *Memoirs*, 1:271.

3. Wollstonecraft, *The Rights of Woman*, p. 261.

4. Thomas Day, *The History of Sandford and Merton* (London: J. Stockdale, 1783–89).

5. Robert Owen, for example, a benevolent reformist-entrepreneur, believed in educating factory children, in lessening labor hours, and improving work conditions. He also argued for a national system of education and viewed character as molded by cultural and physical environment. To alter this situation, he thought this process would have to be (and only could be) understood with the aid of education. See the introduction to Robert Owen, *Report to the Country of Lanark* (London, 1821) and *A New View of Society* (London, 1813–14; reprint. ed., New York: Penguin Books, 1969).

6. Wollstonecraft, *The Rights of Men*, p. 35.

7. Wollstonecraft, *The Rights of Women*, p. 205.

8. Godwin, *Memoirs*, 1:20–21.

9. In *Letters from Sweden*, Wollstonecraft made continual reference to religion. See, for example, letters VII and VIII.

10. Mary Astell, *A Serious Proposal to the Ladies for the Advancement of their Time and Greatest Interest*. Parts 1 and 2.

11. Godwin, *Hints, Posthumous Works*, vol. 4 in vol. 2 pp. 179–95.

12. See Tyson, *Joseph Johnson*, pp. 88–91.

13. Wollstonecraft, *The Rights of Woman*, pp. 220–21.

14. Ibid., pp. 82–83.

15. Godwin, *Memoirs*, 1:283.

16. Alice Rossi, *The Feminist Papers* (New York: Bantam Books, 1974), p. 38.

17. Flexner, *Century of Struggle* (New York: Atheneum, 1973), p. 15.

18. Simone de Beauvoir, *The Second Sex*, trans. and ed. H. M. Parshley (New York: Alfred Knopf, 1952), p. 112.

19. Zillah Eisenstein, *The Radical Future of Liberal Feminism* (New York, London: Longman, 1981), pp. 89–112.

20. Woolf, *The Second Common Reader*, p. 148.

Selected Bibliography

PRIMARY SOURCES

1. Original Works of Mary Wollstonecraft and Modern Editions

The Female Reader; or Miscellaneous-Pieces, in Prose and Verse; Selected from the Best Writers, and Disposed Under Proper Heads; for the Improvement of Young Women. London: Joseph Johnson, 1789. Facsimile. New York: Scholars' Facsimiles & Reprints, 1980.

An Historical and Moral View of the Origin and Progress of The French Revolution, and the Effect it Has Produced in Europe. London: Joseph Johnson, 1794. Facsimile. New York: Scholars' Facsimiles & Reprints, 1975.

Letters Written During a Short Residence in Sweden, Norway, and Denmark. London: Joseph Johnson, 1796. Reprint. Lincoln: University of Nebraska Press, 1976.

Mary, A Fiction. London: Joseph Johnson, 1788. Reprint. New York: Oxford University Press, 1976; New York: Schocken Books, 1977.

Original Stories from Real Life; with Conversations, Calculated to Regulate the Affections, and Form the Mind to Truth and Goodness. London: Joseph Johnson, 1788.

Posthumous Works of the Author of a Vindication of the Rights of Woman, 1798. 2 vols. Dublin: Thomas Burnside, 1798. Facsimile. Fairfield, N.J.: Augustus M. Kelley, 1972; New York: Garland Publishing, 1974.

Thoughts on the Education of Daughters; with Reflections on Female Conduct, in the More Important Duties of Life. London: Joseph Johnson, 1787. Facsimile. New York: Garland Publishing, 1974.

A Vindication of the Rights of Men, in a Letter to the Right Honourable Edmund Burke. London: Joseph Johnson, 1790. Facsimile. New York: Scholars' Facsimiles & Reprints, 1959.

A Vindication of the Rights of Woman with Strictures on Political and Moral Subjects. London: Joseph Johnson, 1792. Reprint. New York: W. W. Norton, 1967, 1975; Penguin Books, 1975.

The Wrongs of Woman: or, Maria. (Part of *Posthumous Works*). Dublin: Thomas Burnside, 1978. Reprint. New York: Oxford University Press, 1976. As *Maria, or the Wrongs of Woman.* New York: W. W. Norton, 1975.

2. Major Collections of Letters
Collected Letters of Mary Wollstonecraft. Edited by Ralph M. Wardle.
Ithaca, London: Cornell University Press, 1979.
Four New Letters of Mary Wollstonecraft and Helen Maria Williams.
Edited by Benjamin P. Kurtz and Carrie C. Autrey. Berkeley: University of California Press, 1937.
Godwin and Mary: Letters of William Godwin and Mary Wollstonecraft.
Edited by Ralph Wardle. Lawrence: University of Kansas Press, 1966.
The Love Letters of Mary Wollstonecraft to Gilbert Imlay, with a Prefatory Memoir. Edited by Roger Ingpen. London: Hutchinson & Co., 1908. Supplement to *Memoirs of Mary Wollstonecraft.* Edited by W. Clark Durant. London: Constable & Co., 1927.
Shelley and His Circle, 1773–1822. Edited by Kenneth Neill Cameron. Cambridge: Harvard University Press, 1961.

3. Selected Writings
A Wollstonecraft Anthology. Bloomington: Indiana University Press, 1977. Includes selections from major works, reviews in the *Analytical Review,* letters, and the essay "On Poetry and Our Relish for the Beauties of Nature."

SECONDARY SOURCES

1. Recent Biographies
Flexner, Eleanor. *Mary Wollstonecraft: A Biography.* New York: Coward, McCann & Geoghegan, 1972. A clear, scholarly account of Wollstonecraft's life with emphasis on the early years and on the emotional patterns created during that time. Several useful appendixes, including those on Edward Wollstonecraft's finances and on the authorship of the reviews in the *Analytical Review.*
George, Margaret. *One Woman's "Situation": A Study of Mary Wollstonecraft.* Urbana: University of Illinois Press, 1970. An incisive political and psychological interpretation of Wollstonecraft's life, stressing the relationship of her experience to her feminism.
Nixon, Edna. *Mary Wollstonecraft: Her Life and Times.* London: J. M. Dent & Sons, 1971. A popular and frequently inaccurate biography retelling the main facts of Wollstonecraft's life.
Sunstein, Emily W. *A Different Face: The Life of Mary Wollstonecraft.* New York: Harper & Row, 1975. A full account of Wollstonecraft's life with psychological comments using Wollstonecraft's fiction for some biographical data. Some discussion of her eighteenth-century context.

Tomalin, Claire. *The Life and Death of Mary Wollstonecraft*. London: Weidenfeld & Nicholson, 1974. A scholarly, witty, but sometimes condescending account of Wollstonecraft's life and social context. Good bibliography.

Wardle, Ralph M. *Mary Wollstonecraft: A Critical Biography*. 1951; Lincoln: University of Nebraska Press, 1966. A good factual biography that deals both with the life and works. Some treatment of Wollstonecraft's contemporaries and of the literary context in which she worked.

2. Some Recent Comments on Wollstonecraft's Life and Works

Boulton, James T. *The Language of Politics in the Age of Wilkes and Burke*. London: Routledge & Kegan Paul, 1963. Treats Wollstonecraft's *Rights of Men* in the context of other eighteenth-century polemical works.

Bouten, Jacob. *Mary Wollstonecraft and the Beginnings of Female Emancipation in France and England*. Amsterdam: H. J. Paris, 1922. Reprint. Philadelphia: Porcupine Press, 1973. Bouten analyses the French and English intellectual influences on Wollstonecraft's thought.

Eisenstein, Zilla. *The Radical Future of Liberal Feminism*. New York: Longman, 1981. Critically analyses Wollstonecraft's place in the development of bourgeois liberal philosophy.

Faderman, Lillian. *Surpassing the Love of Men: Romantic Friendship and Love between Women from the Renaissance to the Present*. New York: William Morrow, 1981. Locates Wollstonecraft's place in the literature of female friendship.,

Fauchery, Pierre. *La Destinée féminine dans le roman européen du dixhuitième siècle 1713–1807*. Paris: Librairie Armand Colin, 1972.

Ferguson, Moira. "The Discovery of Mary Wollstonecraft's *The Female Reader*," *Signs* 5, no. 1 (Summer 1978). Discusses the content and context of *The Female Reader* and includes the original text of Wollstonecraft's preface and four prayers.

——. "Mary Wollstonecraft & Mr. Cresswick," *Philological Quarterly* 1983. Probes the life and relationship to Mary Wollstonecraft of the Cresswick whose name appeared on the title page of *The Female Reader*.

Kelly, Gary. "Godwin, Wollstonecraft and Rousseau," *Women and Literature* 3, no. 2 (1975):21–26. Treats the presence of Rousseau in Wollstonecraft's thought.

——. "Mary Wollstonecraft as Vir Bonus," *English Studies in Canada*

3 (Autumn 1979):275–91. Discusses Wollstonecraft's rhetorical strategies.

Hare, Robert. Introduction to *The Emigrants*. Gainesville: Scholars' Facsimiles & Reprints, 1964. Argues that Wollstonecraft, not Imlay, was the author of *The Emigrants*.

Hickey, Damon. "Mary Wollstonecraft and *The Female Reader*." *English Language Notes* 13 (1975):128–129. Locates and identifies the lost anthology.

Hobman, D. L. *Go Spin, You Jade! Studies in the Emancipation of Woman*. London: Watts, 1957. Summarizes Wollstonecraft's life and educational theories.

Janes, Regina. "Mary, Mary Quite Contrary, Or, Mary Astell and Mary Wollstonecraft Compared," *Studies in Eighteenth Century Culture* 5 (1976):121–39. A suggestive comparison.

————. "On the Reception of Mary Wollstonecraft's *A Vindication of the Rights of Woman*," *Journal of the History of Ideas* 39 (1978): 293–302. Notes the initial favorable reception of Wollstonecraft's major work and the later vilification when her own reputation collapsed.

Loomis, Emerson Robert. "The Godwins in *The Letters of Shahcoolen*," *Nineteenth-Century Fiction* 17 (June 1962):78–80. Discusses *The Letters of Shahcoolen*, an early American attack on Wollstonecraft's life and feminist ideas.

Lundberg, Ferdinand, and Marynia F. Farnham. *Modern Woman: The Lost Sex*. New York: Harper & Brothers, 1947. Attacks Wollstonecraft as mentally ill and deluded.

McAleer, Edward C. *The Sensitive Plant*. Chapel Hill: University of North Carolina Press, 1950. A biography of Margaret, Lady Mountcashel, including a discussion of her relationship with Wollstonecraft.

MacCarthy, B. G. *The Later Women Novelists 1744–1818*. Cork: Cork University Press, 1947. Briefly discusses Wollstonecraft's novels.

Mews, Hazel. *Frail Vessels: Women's Role in Women's Novels from Fanny Burney to George Eliot*. London: Athlone Press, 1969. Comments on Wollstonecraft's pedagogical theories.

Meynell, Alice. "Mary Wollstonecraft's Letters." In *Prose and Poetry*, edited by Frederick Page. London: Jonathan Cape, 1947. Summarizes Wollstonecraft's life and discusses the *Letters to Imlay*.

Moers, Ellen. *Literary Women: The Great Writers*. New York: Doubleday & Co., 1976. Appraises Wollstonecraft's first novel, *Mary, A Fiction*.

Myers, Mitzi. "Mary Wollstonecraft's *Letters Written . . . in Sweden*: Towards Romantic Autobiography," *Studies in Eighteenth-Century Culture* 8 (1979):165–85. Treats Wollstonecraft's travelogue as an account of a mental as well as a physical journey.

Nicholes, Eleanor L. "Mary Wollstonecraft." In *Romantic Rebels, Essays on Shelley and his Circle,* edited by Kenneth Neill Cameron. Cambridge: Harvard University Press, 1973. Concerns Wollstonecraft's literary works, with stress on their personal nature.

Nitchie, Elizabeth. "An Early Suitor of Mary Wollstonecraft." *PMLA* 68 March 1943):163–69. Discusses a possible early romance of Wollstonecraft with Joshua Waterhouse.

Patterson, Sylvia W. *Rousseau's* Emile *and Early Children's Literature.* Metuchen: Scarecrow Press, 1971. Includes a short account of Wollstonecraft's *Original Stories.*

Pénigault-Duhet, P. M. "Du Nouveau sur Mary Wollstonecraft: L'Oeuvre Littéraire de George [sic] Imlay," *Etudes Anglaises* 24 (1971):298–303. Disputes the idea that Wollstonecraft was the author of *The Emigrants,* a novel usually attributed to her lover, Gilbert Imlay.

Peter, Mary. "A Portrait of Mary Wollstonecraft Godwin by John Opie in the Tate Gallery," *Keats-Shelley Memorial Bulletin* 14 (1963): 1–3. Briefly discusses Wollstonecraft and her portrait.

Pollin, Burton R. *Education and Enlightenment in the Works of William Godwin.* New York: Las Americas Publishing Company, 1962. Comments on the influence on Godwin of Wollstonecraft's ideas.

————. "A Federalist Farrago," *Satire Newsletter* 4 (Fall 1966):29–34. Discusses Federalist satire on Wollstonecraft.

————. "Mary Hays on Women's Rights in the *Monthly Magazine,*" *Etudes Anglaises* 24 (1971):271–82. Concerns Mary Hays's attitude toward Wollstonecraft and her review of *Letters from Sweden.*

Rauschenbusch-Clough, Emma. *A Study of Mary Wollstonecraft and the Rights of Women.* London: Longmans, Green, & Co., 1898. Focuses on the intellectual background.

Roper, Derek. "Mary Wollstonecraft's Reviews," *Notes and Queries* 5 1958):37–38. Concerns the authorship of anonymous reviews in the *Analytical Review.*

Rover, Constance. *Love, Morals and the Feminists.* London: Routledge & Kegan Paul, 1970. Describes the lives of major feminists, including Wollstonecraft.

Séjourné, Philippe. *Aspects généraux du roman féminin en Angleterre de 1740 à 1800.* Gap: Louis-Jean, 1966. Discusses Wollstonecraft's novels among those of other contemporary women.

Schnorrenberg, Barbara Brandon. "Thought on the Education of Daughters: The Education of British Girls ca 1750–1850." The Consortium on Revolutionary Europe, Athens, Ga., February, 1982, to be published in their proceedings. This revised view of female education arrived too late to be included.

Stenton, Doris Mary. *The English Woman in History*. London: Allen & Unwin, 1957. Treats Wollstonecraft's life and comments on *The Rights of Woman*, stressing its exaggerated style.

Steeves, Harrison R. *Before Jane Austen: The Shaping of the English Novel in the Eighteenth Century*. London: Allen & Unwin, 1966. Gives critical comments on several of Wollstonecraft's works.

Burke and His Time 16, no. 3 (Spring 1975):271–77. Traces the history of abusive criticism of Wollstonecraft from the eighteenth to the twentieth century.

―――. Mary Wollstonecraft: A Bibliography. New York: Garland Publishing, 1976. Lists 727 items by or concerning Wollstonecraft.

―――. *Women's Friendship in Literature*. New York: Columbia University Press, 1980. Has an interpretation of Wollstonecraft's two novels and their treatment of female relationships.

―――. "Reason and Sensibility in *The Wrongs of Woman*," *Frontiers* 5, no. 3 (Fall 1980):17–20.

Tomkievicz, Shirley. "The First Feminist," *Horizon* 14, no. 2 (Spring 1972):115–19. A short appreciation and biographical summary of Wollstonecraft.

Wardle, Ralph M. "Mary Wollstonecraft, Analytical Reviewer," *PMLA* 62 (December 1947):1000–1009. Concerns Wollstonecraft's contribution to the *Analytical Review*, which Wardle thinks larger than other scholars have accepted.

Welch, Dennis. "Blake's response to Wollstonecraft's *Original Stories*," *Blake: An Illustrated Quarterly* 13, no. 1 (Summer 1979):4–15.

Index

153